Better Homes and Gardens®

Porches

& Sunrooms

YOUR GUIDE TO PLANNING AND REMODELING

Better Homes and Gardens® Books
Des Moines, Iowa

Better Homes and Gardens® Books
An imprint of Meredith® Books

Porches and Sunrooms: Your Guide to Planning and Remodeling
Editor: Paula Marshall
Writer: John Riha
Associate Art Director: Mick Schnepf
Designer: David Jordan
Copy Chief: Catherine Hamrick
Copy and Production Editor: Terri Fredrickson
Book Production Managers: Pam Kvitne, Marjorie J. Schenkelberg
Contributing Copy Editor: Margaret Smith
Contributing Proofreaders: Nancy Dietz, Sue Fetters, Sheila Mauck
Contributing Illustrators and Designers: Carson Ode, Mead Design, The Art Factory
Indexer: Kathleen Poole
Electronic Production Coordinator: Paula Forest
Editorial and Design Assistants: Kaye Chabot, Mary Lee Gavin, Karen Schirm

Meredith® Books
Editor in Chief: James D. Blume
Design Director: Matt Strelecki
Managing Editor: Gregory H. Kayko
Executive Shelter Editor: Denise L. Caringer

Director, Retail Sales and Marketing: Terry Unsworth
Director, Sales, Special Markets: Rita McMullen
Director, Sales, Premiums: Michael A. Peterson
Director, Sales, Retail: Tom Wierzbicki
Director, Sales, Home & Garden Centers: Ray Wolf
Director, Book Marketing: Brad Elmitt
Director, Operations: George A. Susral
Director, Production: Douglas M. Johnston

Vice President, General Manager: Jamie L. Martin

Better Homes and Gardens® **Magazine**
Editor in Chief: Jean LemMon
Executive Building Editor: Joan McCloskey

Meredith Publishing Group
President, Publishing Group: Christopher M. Little
Vice President, Finance & Administration: Max Runciman

Meredith Corporation
Chairman and Chief Executive Officer: William T. Kerr

Chairman of the Executive Committee: E. T. Meredith III

All of us at Better Homes and Gardens® Books are dedicated to providing you with information and ideas to enhance your home. We welcome your comments and suggestions. Write to us at: Better Homes and Gardens® Books, Shelter Editorial Department, 1716 Locust St., Des Moines, IA 50309-3023.

Note to the Reader: Due to differing conditions, tools, and individual skills, Meredith Corporation assumes no responsibility for any damages, injuries suffered, or losses incurred as a result of following the information published in this book. Before beginning any project, review the instructions carefully, and if any doubts or questions remain, consult local experts or authorities. Because local codes and regulations vary greatly, you always should check with local authorities to ensure that your project complies with all applicable local codes and regulations. Always read and observe all of the safety precautions provided by any tool or equipment manufacturer, and follow all accepted safety procedures.

Contents

Evaluate the Possibilities

Answers to often-asked questions guide your choices.

Most houses, regardless of architectural style, can be remodeled to include a porch that makes a graceful transition from the indoor environment to the outdoors or a sunroom that opens up to light and fresh air with large windows and glass doors. Even a small entry portico dramatically alters a home's appearance and expands living space. Renovating these spaces brings back lost charm and adds space to a house, and deserves as much attention to detail as a new addition.

The combination of practicality and aesthetic appeal may explain the revitalized interest in porches and sunrooms, although they have been around for thousands of years. Many people who live in homes without porches or sunrooms now consider adding them. And many homeowners who do have one or the other seek ways to reconfigure, increase the size, or improve the livability with new products and accessories specifically designed to add style and convenience.

Like any home improvement project, adding or renovating these indoor/outdoor spaces is often daunting. This book provides answers and direction. The pages are filled with inspiring ideas for new porches and sunrooms and expert advice so you understand the scope of the work that needs to be done. Before you begin construction, you'll gain a thorough knowledge of basic building codes that may influence the design of your project, the architectural styles that harmonize with your existing house, and the costs that determine what you can get for the budget you can afford. Answers to these and other questions help you explore options and make decisions during the planning process to ensure you get satisfactory results and the most value for your investment dollar.

> ▶ *The wide and welcoming front porch on this 1904 shingle-sided home features classic elements of porch design. The sturdy columns, spaced a generous 8 feet apart, expand the view. The porch floor is painted with durable, weather-resistant enamel, and the ceiling is white to reflect light.*

Contents

Evaluate the Possibilities

Answers to often-asked questions guide your choices.

Most houses, regardless of architectural style, can be remodeled to include a porch that makes a graceful transition from the indoor environment to the outdoors or a sunroom that opens up to light and fresh air with large windows and glass doors. Even a small entry portico dramatically alters a home's appearance and expands living space. Renovating these spaces brings back lost charm and adds space to a house, and deserves as much attention to detail as a new addition.

The combination of practicality and aesthetic appeal may explain the revitalized interest in porches and sunrooms, although they have been around for thousands of years. Many people who live in homes without porches or sunrooms now consider adding them. And many homeowners who do have one or the other seek ways to reconfigure, increase the size, or improve the livability with new products and accessories specifically designed to add style and convenience.

Like any home improvement project, adding or renovating these indoor/outdoor spaces is often daunting. This book provides answers and direction. The pages are filled with inspiring ideas for new porches and sunrooms and expert advice so you understand the scope of the work that needs to be done. Before you begin construction, you'll gain a thorough knowledge of basic building codes that may influence the design of your project, the architectural styles that harmonize with your existing house, and the costs that determine what you can get for the budget you can afford. Answers to these and other questions help you explore options and make decisions during the planning process to ensure you get satisfactory results and the most value for your investment dollar.

▶ *The wide and welcoming front porch on this 1904 shingle-sided home features classic elements of porch design. The sturdy columns, spaced a generous 8 feet apart, expand the view. The porch floor is painted with durable, weather-resistant enamel, and the ceiling is white to reflect light.*

Porches are a great way to give an ordinary house a sense of importance and distinction. To design a porch that is attractive and fits in, look at houses in your neighborhood. Watch for appealing porches on houses similar in size and style to your own. Note key features, such as the overall size of the porch, the style of the posts, and the design of railings. Porches that are well-matched to houses typically have similar features, such as matching roofing materials and trim. Flip through magazines and books to get ideas (see Creating Architectural Harmony, pages 90–91). To create a fitting porch,

BEFORE

▲ This ordinary 1984 suburban house languished on the market for months before it was bought by an architect who knew just what it needed—a front porch, opposite, to connect the house to its surroundings. An entry porch, above, completed the changes.

you'll likely need an architect to develop your plans, so it makes sense to find one at the beginning. Share your ideas and get the architect's advice on design and materials.

As you plan, you may find it helpful to try out your ideas on paper. Begin with an elevation drawing of your house, and make photocopies of it to experiment with designs. These sketches create a good basis for talking about what you want with an architect and, later, with a builder.

You'll need working drawings to present to the local building department for approval; unless you are well-versed in architectural design, you'll need an architect to translate your ideas to working drawings. You also need these finished drawings for a building contractor to order materials and begin work. Once you're satisfied, your architect will produce a complete set of drawings for your project (see Working with a Design Professional, pages 91–93).

> ➤ *Bumping out into the backyard provided plenty of room for this 12×32-foot, four-season sunroom addition. It is a bit of good fortune that the back of the house faces south—perfect for capturing the winter sunlight.*

Q *How do I know if I have the space in my yard for an addition?*

Size and configuration of your project are determining factors. A wraparound front porch could easily fit in the front yard yet intrude on local setback ordinances where it turns the corner and as it continues along the side of your home.

First, check with your community's building and planning department about the restrictions that apply to your property (see Understanding Your Property, pages 89–90). A typical setback requirement, for example, of 15 feet in from the sides of your property lines, and 45 feet from either front or back property lines, may restrict the placement and size of your desired new porch or sunroom.

Another important consideration in any new project is the existing landscape. Think about what alterations are necessary—what plants and trees, if any, could be lost, or how to cope with building on a steep slope. Certain features—such as a large tree or valuable plantings—may require a change in the shape of your design.

Also remember that sunrooms need proper orientation to the sun to create the desired effect (see Elements of Style–Sunrooms, pages 60–85).

Q *What's the difference between a three-season porch and a sunroom? Aren't both enclosed?*

While both are enclosed, the main difference is that a sunroom includes fully insulated walls and ceiling, insulated-glass windows, and systems to provide both heating and cooling, similar to any room of your house (see Finding Your Style, pages 16–37). A sunroom can remain open to the main house at any time of the year or any time of day. During winter, a properly oriented sunroom acts as a solar collector, gaining and storing heat from sunlight. A sunroom is moderately more expensive to construct than a three-season porch of similar size.

A three-season porch typically uses less expensive components, such as uninsulated-glass windows and doors. Although it is delightful during sunny spring and fall days, at these times of the year it loses heat rapidly at night. For this reason, a three-season porch should be separated from the main house by insulated walls or doors with insulated glass. On cold winter days, even the warmth of a bright sun will not be enough to heat a three-season porch to comfortable temperatures.

▼ *Replacing old, single-pane windows with insulated-glass windows and adding insulation in the walls and ceiling turned this lofty, second-story three-season porch into a cozy, year-round sunspace.*

Q Don't sunrooms get excessively hot during summer?

Well-planned sunrooms typically employ several strategies to prevent them from getting too hot. For example, many windows and skylights have optional features, such as built-in shades and surface coatings, that are designed to control solar gain (see Planning with a Purpose, pages 86–97). Also, sunshine and heat can be controlled with window shades or blinds designed to enhance the interior decor. Fan-assisted ventilation, controlled by a thermostat, ensures that a sunroom will receive fresh, cool air even when you are not at home. In addition, a well-planned sunroom takes advantage of trees and leafy vines for shading and is oriented to reduce the amount of direct sun during the hottest times of the year.

➤ *With so many windows, air-conditioning is a must to make this sunroom comfortable in the summer months. Also, plenty of shade from deciduous trees, openable windows, and a ceiling fan to stir the air keep the room comfortable.*

Q *I'd like my porch to have style, but aren't my choices limited when it comes to weatherproof furnishings?*

On the contrary, you'll find an incredible variety of weatherproof and weather-resistant furniture and fabrics, thanks to an increase in demand for stylish outdoor furnishings (see Furnishing with Style, pages 98–105). Some classic standbys, such as painted wicker rockers, willow twig chairs and tables, and teak benches, for centuries have proven themselves to be as durable as they are beautiful. New generations of furniture materials, such as look-alike wicker made of vinyl-coated wire or furnishings of anodized aluminum that mimic wrought iron, are guaranteed to last for many years with little maintenance. Many acrylic fabrics are designed to withstand the toughest conditions without fading or loss of strength. Even some of your favorite cotton fabrics can be laminated to withstand harsh weather. Ask about the process at your local fabric store.

Q *I'd like to add a screen porch. Do I need railings, or can I just have screen panels?*

Local building codes vary, however, most specify railings at least 36 inches high on decks that are more than 30 inches off the ground. This applies to screen porches, too, which may be thought of as enclosed decks. One way to comply with codes and create a good-looking screen porch is to build low walls—knee walls—around the perimeter of the porch. These solid walls satisfy railing requirements. Knee walls have the added benefit of raising the height of your screen material, which helps prevent damage to the screen. A framing member at the required height may be sufficient to meet code and create an open look.

▶ *Simple construction is well-suited to the screen porch of this vacation home. The supporting 2×4-foot studs are exposed from floor to ceiling. The bottom portion of the walls are filled in with 36-inch-high wood panels—tall enough to be code-compliant safety railings yet still permit plenty of fresh air and wide-open views.*

Q *What's the best placement for a sunroom?*

The orientation of the sunroom may be a compromise between vistas and sunlight control. Ideally, a sunroom should have at least one south-facing wall (a hexagon- or octagon-shape sunroom could have two southern-exposure walls) to take advantage of winter sun in northern climates. A sunroom that occupies the southeast corner of a home, with window walls facing south and east, is ideal. That way, it captures early morning sun when temperatures are mild throughout the year and avoids late evening summertime sun when excess heat gain is a problem. Outfit a sunroom with shades or blinds to give full control over the amount of sun that reaches the interior.

Familiarity with your particular situation is helpful—if you've lived in your house for a year or two, you probably have a good idea of how sunlight falls at all times of the year. With the correct orientation, a sunroom is likely to provide welcome daylight to increase the enjoyment of your home.

Another factor is the orientation toward exterior views. If you're lucky enough to have good scenery surrounding your home, position your sunroom for the most advantageous view.

Privacy is often an issue with a room composed mostly of glass. You'll want to be sure that your sunroom isn't open to the plain view of neighbors or passersby, and that it doesn't intrude on your neighbor's sense of privacy, either.

▲ *This small, south-facing sun pavilion is positioned to capture early morning light. If the morning sun is too strong, however, there's a canvas awning for shade.*

▶ *Restoring this magnificent, 1870s Victorian wouldn't be complete without repairing the grand porch. Old photos from the local historical society helped when designing historically accurate details.*

Q Can I add a porch to my historic house?

That likely depends on the definition of historic house. Some cities have historic districts, and the term "historic house" is an official designation that carries legal obligations to the owner of such a property for preserving the look of the house, especially the exterior. Alterations typically are strictly controlled by a local historic committee that reviews any proposed changes to homes within its jurisdiction. If you have no such designation for your home, it's still a good idea to engage the services of an architect or professional designer to ensure your new porch is architecturally compatible with your home and neighborhood.

First, determine if your home falls within these guidelines. If it does, you might want to do some investigating. Many older houses had porches at one time, and research at your local library or historical society may reveal photographs that show your house with such an embellishment. If so, you'll have evidence of a historic precedent that may persuade a historic review committee to allow a porch to be constructed. However, the committee may limit the design to what is seen in old photographs.

Also, your house or property may display physical evidence of having a porch at an earlier date. Markings or shadows of details, such as posts or railings, indicate that an original porch was removed sometime in the past. This evidence may persuade the historic review committee to allow the construction of a new porch. If your house doesn't have evidence of a previously existing porch, look through books devoted to historic residential architecture to discover houses similar to your own that include porches. Use any of these avenues to develop a convincing argument.

Finding Your Style

Imaginative living spaces connect interiors to the out-of-doors.

The word *porch* instantly conjures images of creaking rocking chairs, mild summer breezes, and glasses of lemonade. Porches take many forms, however, each as individual as the people who create them. A porch may be as simple as a roofed-over deck or as elaborate as an Italianate portico. When fully enclosed, it is a sunroom that includes insulated walls and ceilings, insulated-glass windows and doors, and a heating and cooling system. Both porches and sunrooms are designed to gather daylight and fresh air and place occupants in proximity to the surrounding nature.

The design of your porch or sunroom depends on a careful evaluation of your needs and your budget. You might want a cozy getaway space that allows you to enjoy evening sunsets in privacy. In that case, a small porch attached to the back of your house may be sufficient. If you're considering a serious architectural upgrade for your home's facade, an expansive, wraparound porch is an open invitation to gracious outdoor living.

If you envision summer entertaining on your new porch, position it in proximity to your kitchen and make sure it's enclosed with screened panels to keep annoying insects at bay. If you look forward to enjoying the sun's warmth even in winter, build a year-round sunroom.

Porches and sunrooms are fun, casual spaces. They allow the natural environment to be a part of everyday living and have the potential to be one of the most delightful areas of your home. With careful planning, you can take advantage of a porch or sunroom's special characteristics while adding new ideas that increase your home's livability and value.

▲ This all-season porch features sliding windows. During warm weather, windows and doors open to create a virtual screen porch. Tongue-and-groove ceiling planks and wicker furniture give the space a porchlike feel throughout the year.

Basic Options for Style

Porch and sunroom designs fall into four basic styles. Each style can be evaluated in terms of cost, complexity, and exposure to the elements. When planning your project, start with one of the basic designs, then customize it to suit your needs and tastes. For more inspiration, you'll find plenty of ideas in the many variations of these basic styles on the following pages of this chapter.

Open Porch

The open porch is a classic, first gaining popularity with North American homeowners during the late 1800s and influencing home design for several decades. Designed as an element of social interaction, the front-facing porch lost favor during the last half of the 20th century, replaced in part by backyard decks and patios that offer more privacy.

The open porch is basically a deck covered by a roof structure supported by posts. It may be elevated or near ground level. Street-facing versions typically feature wide, welcoming stairways and perimeter railings as part of the overall entrance scheme. Large porches may incorporate more than one doorway, giving interiors added dimension and possibilities. On the complexity and material requirements scale, this is one of the easiest porches to design and construct.

Screen Porch

A screen porch differs from the open porch with the addition of perimeter walls of large screened panels that allow fresh air to circulate but help keep out bugs. Creating a screen porch is a fairly inexpensive way to expand living space and to enjoy the outdoors. It's typical to vacation home construction,

Open Porch

Screen Porch

▲ *Built at ground level, this sunny open porch features a durable, easy-to-clean patio-style brick floor. The design invites nearby flowers and shrubs to be an integral part of the porch environment. Pairs of columns and floral borders on the ceiling add design flair.*

▲ *With sconces and a delicate chandelier, this screen porch is ready for evening entertaining. Built in Florida, this space is enjoyed year-round.*

where use of the porch is often limited to summer months and more elaborate enclosure is unnecessary. The screen porch often has a casual, comfortable, unpretentious feel. As with an open porch, a screen porch offers little or no security, so furnishings and accessories tend to be lightweight and mobile to be moved indoors at the end of the porch-sitting season.

Three-Season Porch

The three-season porch is designed to extend a home's usable living area with a minimum of expense. By enclosing an existing solid-floor porch area with partial walls, screens, glazed windows, and a door, a homeowner gains use of the porch during inclement weather and chilly spring or fall days. A portable space heater, for a low additional cost, lengthens the use of a three-season porch.

Popular in the 1960s and 1970s, the three-season porch is increasingly obsolete. Low-cost insulated-glass windows and doors, and the relative simplicity of adding insulation and surface finishes to walls and ceilings have made sunrooms a more cost-effective and practical choice.

Sunroom

A sunroom is characterized by fully insulated walls and ceilings, generous use of insulated-glass windows and doors, and thermostatically controlled heating and cooling systems. Although a sunroom may be composed almost entirely of glass, it is designed for warmth and comfort even on the coldest days. A sunroom invites as much natural daylight as possible into the home and has a minimum of structural elements, such as walls or posts, that block light or views. Sunrooms usually are not separated from main living areas by doors. Exceptions are sunrooms used as greenhouses or when security is a concern. Because sunrooms are regular rooms, they usually are the most expensive option a homeowner may consider when adding a porchlike environment to the home.

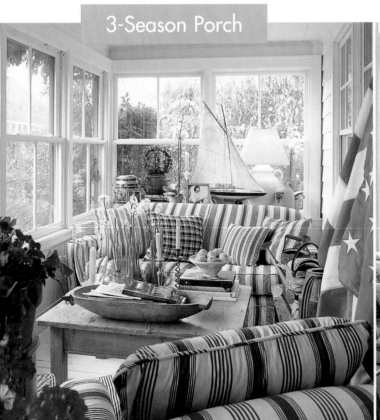

3-Season Porch

Sunroom

▲ *There's abundant living space tucked into this narrow, front-facing three-season porch. Plenty of sun-gathering glass makes this a comfortable room in all but the coldest weather.*

▲ *Built to enclose a portion of an existing patio garden, this casual sunroom features brick floors that mimic the backyard walkways. Comfy armchairs and a pair of child's chairs invite the family to enjoy garden views.*

▲ *Spacious and elegant, this top-of-the-line conservatory, above and opposite, features polished marble floors and curved insulated glass. The furnishings are a refined mix of upholstered pieces and exquisite antiques.*

Elegance Under Glass

Conservatories are glassed-in sunrooms that frequently feature exceptional quality and fine details. They were popular in 18th- and 19th-century England where the mild, but often damp, climate made them a practical way to extend the outdoor season. They typically were used to grow plants in proximity to living spaces and often were referred to by the fanciful name *orangerie*—a place to grow orange trees. Although the methods of their construction are similar to the manufacturing of simpler, prefabricated conservatory sunrooms (see Installing a Prefab Sunroom, pages 82–85), the finest versions use exceptional materials, such as hardwood frames and curved glass for roofs. Expect to pay a premium price for a high-end conservatory. Depending on the size, these conservatories range from $20,000 to $100,000, installed.

Like any ancillary structure that is attached to a main house, a conservatory must be supported by a full perimeter foundation that extends below the frost line. After the foundation is installed, the construction is a straightforward assembly of parts.

Conservatories tend to be tall structures, often 15 feet or higher at the peak, giving them a large interior volume that needs to be considered when planning supplemental heating and cooling. Because they are all-glass structures, cooling a conservatory to comfortable temperatures in the warmest months is a big job. Most companies offer roller shades built into the roof rafters as an option.

Consult with a heating and cooling specialist about your particular needs. An additional system, such as a small heat pump, is required to handle the heating and cooling demands of a large conservatory. To grow plants in a conservatory, plan for water-resistant flooring, such as ceramic tile, and easy access to water, such as an exterior-style spigot. If the conservatory is unheated, install a frost-proof spigot.

The Ever-Gracious Gazebo

A gazebo usually refers to a free-standing, decorative garden structure. While most gazebos conform to this definition, the graceful shape and beautiful style of the gazebo can be adapted as a sitting porch. Created as an extension of an existing porch, or connected to interior rooms by a short, covered passageway, the gazebo is an exceptionally fun and useful structure that lends itself to furniture groups for casual entertaining or for relaxing with the family on a summer evening.

The multisided shape and independent, conical roof of a gazebo requires clever design and careful planning to ensure it integrates well with the overall design of your house. Existing porch fascia, trim details, railing configuration, and color schemes should be extended to an attached gazebo so that it has the appearance of having been part of the original design of your house. Historically, gazebos are associated with English Tudor and Victorian designs. An imaginative architect, however, should be able to design a gazebo that is appropriate for your house.

An attached gazebo can be treated as an open porch or enclosed with screens (see Screening Options, pages 48–49) to create a relaxing, bug-free haven. To ensure comfort, consider running electricity to power lights, a ceiling fan, stereo equipment, or even a small refrigerator in your gazebo. Be sure to install a ground fault circuit interrupter (GFCI) device in the line at the main electrical panel. A GFCI device interrupts current at the slightest hint of a malfunction or short circuit and is an especially good safety feature for outdoor environments. According to the National Electrical Code, all receptacles in the gazebo should be of the GFCI variety.

▲ *When the owners of this 1887 Victorian house, inset above, decided to add a screen porch, they consulted an architect. The result is a multi-sided gazebo attached to the house by a screened breezeway. The style is an elegant architectural fit for this beautiful historic house.*

An American Classic

The front-facing porch hearkens to the late 19th and early 20th centuries, when most North American homes featured a wide and welcoming front facade. At that time, porches were part of the social fabric, connecting homeowners and families with the streets and surrounding neighborhoods. As street traffic increased, making vehicle noise more intrusive, the sitting porch migrated to the rear of the house, away from passing cars and trucks. Although the move makes sense, it led to several generations of houses that favored backyard patios or decks over front-facing porches.

Today the trend is reversing. Front-facing porches that add living area and provide an emotional investment in the surrounding community are increasingly popular projects. These additions also prove to be sound financial investments by creating homes with plenty of charm and curb appeal. Many newly built homes reflect traditional design based on familiar and comforting motifs, such as the Midwestern farmhouse and the shingle-sided seaside home of the Northeast. These new homes often include porches—large, covered rooms thoughtfully integrated into the overall design.

> ▶ *Curvaceous railing balusters add a touch of elegance to the porch of this renovated older home. Note how solid, square sections of railing support the round columns. This detail allows the railing to be fitted against a flat surface instead of the round one.*

When planning a front-facing porch, its style and dimensions are primary considerations. Because it's a prominent feature, you want it to be a seamless addition, looking as if it were an original part of your home. For this reason, consider hiring an architect or other qualified design professional to ensure your porch is well-matched to your house (see Planning with a Purpose, pages 86–97). A designer should advise you whether your house would look better with a simple entry porch or with no porch at all. For example, many colonial-style houses, such as the saltbox, are designed to have a forthright, austere appearance. If architectural integrity is important,

consider the visual impact a porch will have on your home.

The front-facing porch usually is attached directly to a house without modifications to siding, windows, or doors. For a long porch, consider an

additional doorway to create access from another room, but make sure you can live with the changes in interior traffic patterns. Prefabricated porch posts, railings, balusters, and decorative brackets and trim made of wood or polyurethane are available at most home improvement centers. Choose the parts that are appropriate to the style of your home. If you don't see appropriate parts on display, ask to see manufacturers' catalogs for parts that can be special ordered.

▶ *Broad, front-facing porches characterize this turn-of-the-century neighborhood in St. Louis. Friendly porches were integral to the social interaction of communities, inviting passersby to stop and chat at a time when foot traffic was common.*

Wrapped in Delight

The wraparound porch is a variation of the classic front-facing porch. In this form, the porch runs along a portion of at least two sides of the house. It was popular on Victorian-style farmhouses and shingle-style bungalows of the late 19th and early 20th centuries. In terms of convenience, a two-sided porch offers flexibility. You can easily move in and out of shifting sunlight and prevailing winds, and you have a choice of views. Sit at the front if you like to watch the street-side activity, or situate yourself on the side for privacy.

A large wraparound porch accommodates two entrances to the house. A second stairway for a side entry is common. If you are considering a wraparound porch, plan carefully before committing to another entrance; make it a convenience—not a busy thoroughfare through what was once a quiet interior sitting area. A good example is a separate entrance to provide direct access to a master suite or an apartment. For a second entry, be sure to make the distinction between the primary, public entrance and the secondary, more private doorway. Avoid confusion with a main walkway and stairs that lead clearly and directly to the front door.

When adding a wraparound porch, a primary consideration is the setback requirement. It may not be an issue for the front-facing portion of the porch, but typically the sides of homes are closer to lot lines, especially on urban or suburban lots. Be sure to check the setback requirements in your area by calling your local building or planning department (see The Basics of Building, pages 106–111).

▶ *A gracefully curved wraparound porch is an eye-catching feature of this 1894 Queen Anne Victorian home. This beauty demonstrates the classic language of porch architecture—a small, front-facing gable in the porch roof draws attention to the main stairs and primary entry.*

▲ Shingle-style homes of the Northeast often feature generous wraparound porches. The porch of this renovated 1910 Massachusetts home faces the ocean. In the parlance of seaside homes, that means the porch is on the front of the house.

▲ Inspired by the style of Craftsman-era homes, this newly built California house features a wraparound porch that completely encircles the structure.

Making a Grand Entrance

▲ *When it came to renovating this 1970s rambler, a fresh look for the entry was a priority. A new brick walkway leading to a gable-end porch supported by classical columns makes a grand statement. A curved ceiling for the porch adds a dash of high style.*

Porches needn't be large to be useful and appealing. Even a small entry porch—sometimes called a portico—provides shelter from the elements for visitors at the door, creates a comfortable area for sitting outdoors, and enhances the curb appeal of your home, all for minimal cost. Because the material requirements are minimal, consider using top-quality components such as finely made posts and moldings.

Although the entry porch is an especially simple addition, resist the temptation to use an existing concrete stoop or apron to support the new structure unless you've examined it carefully. Newer houses—those no more than 15 years old—may have stoops or concrete steps that have been poured as integral parts of your home's perimeter foundation. If this is the case, its foundation will extend beyond the frost line and will provide adequate support.

Older homes, however, may have stoops or concrete steps that were poured separately from the home's foundation. As a result, they will probably shift with seasonal changes. Even slight settling may result in expensive damage to your new entry porch. An older stoop should be removed and a new concrete foundation installed, complete with piers that extend below the frost line in accordance with local building codes.

As with any porch, an entry porch or portico should harmonize with the architectural style of your home: Include similar trim details, roofing materials, roof pitch, and color key it to your house. Entry porches with more than two steps or higher than 30 inches from the ground require railings, as specified by local building codes. If the entry porch does not encompass existing exterior lighting fixtures, plan to provide lighting on the walls or in the ceiling of the new structure.

In harsh climates, consider enclosing the entry porch with windows and a storm door. This type of protection doesn't require insulated glass or supplemental heating; a three-season design is adequate for providing a sheltered area for removing wet or muddy boots and stowing umbrellas.

◀ *A simple, functional portico is a welcome addition for this colonial-style house. The tastefully designed entry is topped with a flat roof and a small, nonfunctional balcony. Other possibilities include curved or peaked roofs.*

Two-Story Porches
Are a Cut Above

Not all porches or sunrooms are just a single story high. Some rise vertically, providing new vistas and private sitting areas for upper-level rooms. The two-story porch has its origins in homes of the 18th and 19th centuries, when air-conditioning was unknown and catching an outdoor breeze was the only relief from summer heat. Examples are porches on the Classic and Greek Revival homes popular during the mid-1800s. These types of houses often featured entryways protected by soaring porches topped with large, triangular roofs called pediments. Sometimes, the tall porch columns also supported small balconies looking out from upstairs bedrooms. This Revival design frequently is copied by suburban homes today.

Enclosing an old porch and adding another story serves multiple purposes. The lower level provides room for an apartment. The upper level becomes a sunroom for the master bedroom.

Adding a two-story porch or sunroom is a good way to increase valuable living space while conserving expenses. The savings come from minimizing the foundation—it supports both the first and second levels of additional living area. If the same amount of square footage were spread out on a single level, the overall costs would increase significantly because of the more extensive foundation work required.

A two-story porch or sunroom offers many enticing options. For example, the lower portion could be a screened sitting porch and the upper level a fully insulated bedroom, bath, or home office. Another possibility is to make the upper portion a screened sleeping porch for balmy nights, while the lower portion is a fully enclosed sunroom. Whatever your priorities, building a two-story addition is a substantial project that must be planned carefully to blend with the style of your home.

A soaring, two-story screen porch allows the owners of this newly built home to enjoy bug-free, cooling breezes and lofty views of the Kankakee River in Illinois.

Often this type of project means extending an existing roof or having a new roof intersect the old one, providing additional gutters and downspouts, and making sure the new roof is adequately ventilated to prevent moisture buildup in the roof framing system. Also, both levels should be natural extensions of existing living space. These considerations generally mean contracting the services of a registered architect or other design professional who can handle complex design issues and produce imaginative results (see Working with a Design Professional, pages 91–93).

A two-story, front-facing porch takes historical precedent from the Classic Revival houses of the 19th century. This newly built home also features a wraparound porch along the lower level.

Add-On Sunshine

One of the most convenient ways to bring generous amounts of light into the home is with a prefabricated sunroom. The simplest versions of these types of structures come ready-made from the factory and are designed to attach directly to the home with few modifications to the existing siding. They are available in many sizes, shapes, and configurations to complement the architectural style of most homes. Most manufacturers also fulfill custom orders of sunrooms to fit unusual shapes or configurations.

Because it is attached to your home, most building codes require a sunroom to have a perimeter foundation that provides support below the frost line. After the foundation is constructed and the concrete has cured, a prefabricated sunroom often is installed in only a few days.

An advantage of prefabricated sunrooms is the number of options available from the manufacturers. Select from wood or aluminum frames; conventional or glass roofs; variable roof pitches, wall heights, and glazing options that include insulated glass, mirrored glass, and insulated glass with inert gas fillings; and built-in shades. Match these options to your particular climate and building site. Some components, such as solid roof or floor panels, are already insulated and feature prefinished surfaces and snap-together seams that make installation fast, easy, and cost-effective.

To use your sunroom year-round, plan for supplemental heating and cooling. This can be an extension of your existing system or independent units—such as electric baseboard heaters and window air-conditioning units (see Heating and Cooling, pages 65–69).

Stretching nearly 40 feet along the side of the house, an 11-foot-deep, prefabricated sunspace serves as both a greenhouse and a living area. Three sets of French doors open to the home's living room, providing daylight and plentiful, expansive views.

Patios That Are Never Bugged

If you have a ground-level backyard patio, consider enclosing a portion of it with a simple structure with a roof and walls with screen panels. Screened enclosures set directly on grade level are a great way to increase your backyard enjoyment while avoiding pesky bugs (see Screening Options, pages 48–49). You won't need to install flooring—it's already there. Brick, crushed rock, flagstone, or a concrete slab all work well for grade-level enclosures. The building codes in most areas, however, require that ancillary structures attached to houses be supported by perimeter foundations that extend below the frost line. An existing concrete slab typically includes a perimeter footing that will provide adequate support. In other instances, you will need to excavate the perimeter of the proposed structure and install a code-compliant foundation. If you are unsure, have a remodeling contractor, architect, or other qualified building professional inspect your patio.

Screened structures sitting at grade level are not required by codes to provide safety railings, so the design and construction can be relatively straightforward. Vertical support members, such as 4×4s or 6×6s spaced 4 feet on-center, with removable screen panels set in between, are commonly used as the basis for design. Although not required by building codes, a horizontal safety rail, set 30 to 36 inches from the floor, prevents accidental damage to the screen.

▶ *Although simple in design and construction, this screen porch achieves architectural interest with a large semicircular screened opening in the gable end. The foundation is a new concrete slab installed in the middle of an existing brick patio. The unfinished concrete floors are covered with jute rugs and are easy to sweep clean.*

When the owners of this Atlanta home wanted to renovate an attic into a master suite, they were stumped about where to locate the stairs. The solution was a stair tower added to the back of the house. The middle landing, below, *became a light-filled sunspace with a small balcony overlooking the yard.*

Creating Sunny Nooks

Make a sun-filled space without adding an entire room. By installing banks of windows and glass doors in smaller areas, you introduce light and fresh air to the interior of your home. Small nooks like this can light up a corridor, enliven a kitchen, or bathe a stairway landing in daylight. Instead of a full sunroom, consider a sunspace that appears as a bright surprise in your home.

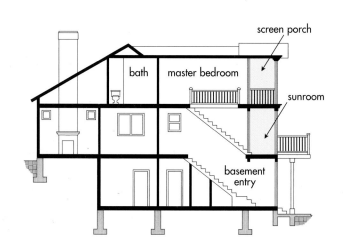

screen porch

bath | master bedroom

sunroom

basement entry

A good time to consider a sunspace is when planning a remodeling project. If you are adding new walls, imagine how they might look if they were made mostly of windows. Naturally, you'll want to consider all aspects of opening up your home with glass—orientation to the sun at different times of the day and year, privacy, and views. Safety is another issue. If small children are present, limit floor-to-ceiling expanses of glass with low knee walls or by breaking up banks of windows with horizontal framing members located about 30 inches from the floor.

Like sunrooms, sunspaces take advantage of the latest innovations in window and door technology by creating beautiful, glassed-in areas that are well insulated against heat loss. Windows with special coatings designed to reflect heat back into rooms, high-performance glazings, and dead-air spaces filled with inert gases, such as argon, have especially good insulating capabilities—nearly as good as solid stud walls built just 20 years ago.

Doors and skylights also have benefited from the technology that has improved energy performance in building components.

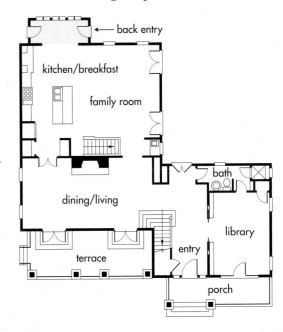

The image shows a floor plan with the following labels: back entry, kitchen/breakfast, family room, bath, dining/living, library, entry, terrace, porch.

▲ *Enclosing the underside of a small balcony at the rear of this house,* top, *created a sunny mudroom,* above, *that opens to the renovated kitchen. This all-season porch adds abundant light.*

Elements of Style
Porches

Becoming familiar with surfaces and materials.

To turn the porch of your dreams into reality, gain a thorough understanding of all the components and how they are assembled. To begin, you'll need to decide where to build access to your porch from inside, choose the size and style of any windows and doors, and select materials for flooring, walls, and ceilings. And you'll need to choose the style of stairs, railings, and any architectural details that will embellish the final design. Making these decisions early helps your project proceed smoothly and efficiently.

Familiarize yourself with the available options to make the wisest choices for both style and budget. Some elements, such as wood posts and railings, offer unmatched beauty and crisp details, and require periodic maintenance. Other materials are expensive and can have a significant impact on your budget. To help you set and maintain a budget, make firm decisions about surfaces and finishes before you begin your project.

If you work with a design professional, having definite ideas about the appearance of your porch helps the professional understand your needs, create solutions, and avoid problems. To communicate clearly, keep a scrapbook of ideas. Cut pictures from magazines and collect product brochures that illustrate colors, the materials, or the quality of workmanship that you expect.

Porches are distinctive living spaces because they are exposed to heat, cold, sun, rain, and even snow. Select weather-resistant materials and finishes that are especially designed to withstand season after season of harsh climactic conditions. Many kinds of materials, such as ceramic tile, come in quality levels to suit any budget.

◄ The owners of this three-season porch got the maximum style by using readily available materials. Staining walls and rafters dark and painting the trim and ceiling a soft yellow adds drama and flair for little cost. Matchstick blinds help control sunlight.

Anatomy of a Porch

Porches appear to be a less complex structure than they are: They have many components that serve specific purposes (see *below*). It's a good idea to have a basic understanding of porch construction and terminology so you can communicate effectively with an architect, a building contractor, and the other professionals involved in the design and construction of your porch.

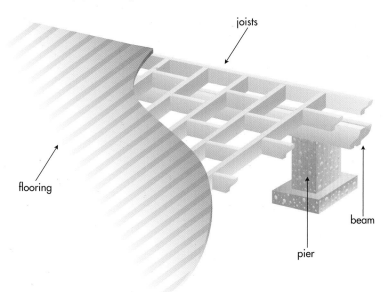

joists

flooring

beam

pier

PORCH TERMS

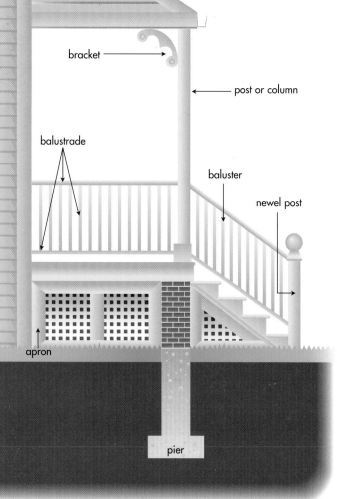

bracket

post or column

balustrade

baluster

newel post

apron

pier

Foundations

Any structure, such as a porch, attached directly to your house is required to have a concrete foundation that complies with local building codes. The foundation footing must be deeper than the frost line, typically 36 to 48 inches below grade. This prevents the foundation from moving when the soil expands and contracts as it freezes during colder months.

There are three types of foundations for porches. The most common is the pier foundation (see *above*)—poured concrete shafts spaced at regular intervals throughout the porch area. Piers sometimes are designed as columns that extend above ground to support the floor joists and girders—the porch substructure. The above-ground portion of the piers is then veneered with brick or stone for an attractive appearance. Occasionally, piers stop at grade level and pressure-treated wood posts support the substructure. Decorative lattice, called an apron, often fills the spaces between piers or posts.

Other types of foundations include solid poured concrete or concrete block walls that are veneered with brick, stone, or stucco. This method uses more materials and is more labor-intensive, making it a more expensive option. It often is used for houses that have masonry siding so that the new foundation can blend seamlessly with the existing materials.

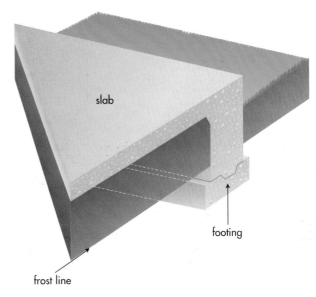

Solid foundation walls need small vents to promote air circulation and prevent moisture from building up underneath the porch.

To build a porch at grade level, use a slab foundation (see *right*). Slabs can be covered with a variety of top-quality finish materials including brick, ceramic tile, or cut stone. Any framing members that come in direct contact with the slab need to be pressure-treated wood.

Substructures and Floors

The substructure of a wood-frame porch is similar to a simple deck (see page 42). The heaviest support members—the beams (sometimes called girders)—support floor joists. Flooring or decking is installed directly over the joists. To prevent rot, it's a good idea to create a substructure of pressure-treated wood.

As with a deck, a key framing member is the ledger—the piece of lumber installed directly against the house. The ledger usually is bolted in place with heavy galvanized bolts or lag screws. To prevent moisture and debris from getting between the ledger and the house, the top seam should be

SLAB FOUNDATION

slab

footing

frost line

41

existing house wall

ledger board

steel joist hangers

porch deck

floor joist

blocking

carefully sealed with caulk or covered with galvanized metal flashing.

Because a porch is exposed to the elements, the floor must shed water. This means designing the substructure so that the floor gently slopes away from the house. A typical slope would be a drop of about ¼ inch for every horizontal foot of decking. Therefore, a 10-foot-wide porch would have a built-in slope of 2½ inches. This can create some challenging problems for the builder, who must custom-fit posts between the sloped floor and the level roofline above. Some builders also insist that wood flooring be installed with the seams between boards running perpendicular to the side of the house, allowing water to drain directly toward the outside edge of the porch.

Posts and Railings

Posts support the roof; the railing system—called a balustrade—runs between the posts. Local building codes determine the minimum size and the spacing of the posts. After that, it's a matter of aesthetics. The size and spacing of posts should be in harmony with the architectural style of your house and the overall look of your porch addition. Similarly, the balustrade must comply with codes and should be designed as an integral element of the overall porch design. Most codes specify a distance of not greater than 4 inches between balusters.

Some houses, especially older homes, feature solid walls instead of railings. This is common with shingle-style homes and bungalows, where the porch is surrounded by a low shingled wall and posts are set atop the wall. Solid walls should include scuppers—holes set at floor level to encourage drainage.

> *Although the porch of this 1930s bungalow is built on a wood foundation, the steps are concrete and the perimeter walls and columns are solid brick. The decorative arches in the solid walls are scuppers— holes designed to permit drainage.*

Roofs

The roof structure is another element that should harmonize with the existing architectural style of the house. Similar fascia details, colors, and roofing materials help integrate a new porch with the house.

Like the floor framing system, the roof framing attaches to the house with a ledger. Care must be taken so that the seam between the house siding and the porch roof is sealed against leaks with flashing (see *below*)—a thin galvanized metal strip typically bent in an L shape. One leg of the flashing installs under existing siding and the other extends over the top of the new porch roofing.

The area under the roof may be left open, exposing the framing members to view from below, or enclosed. Enclosed framing has two versions: vaulted ceilings include finish materials that cover the roof rafters; a drop ceiling features ceiling joists installed horizontally and designed to carry a finish ceiling material such as wood or drywall. The classic porch ceiling material—beaded board—is a popular choice and is available as individual boards, plywood sheets, polyurethane, and aluminum panels.

Certain amenities, such as ceiling fans and lighting fixtures, install easily in porch ceilings. Plan to run the necessary wiring in the cavity between the finish ceiling and the roof.

ROOF FLASHING

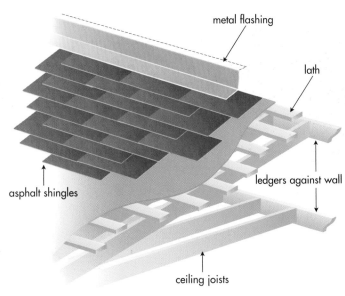

metal flashing

lath

asphalt shingles

ledgers against wall

ceiling joists

Flooring

A porch floor should be beautiful, durable, and, above all, resistant to moisture. It should not warp, splinter, or chip, and it should provide a smooth, safe walking surface that is free from defects. Flooring choices are influenced by the type of porch foundation. Wood floors typically are used with post-and-pier foundations that have a substructure of beams and joists. Ceramic tile, cut stone, and brick usually are reserved for slab foundations. Tile and stone, however, can be used on elevated porches, providing the substructure is designed to withstand the considerable weight, the subfloor has been properly prepared, and the floor is pitched to shed water. Indoor-outdoor carpets install over either wood or concrete slabs.

Wood Floors

Years ago, porch floors traditionally were made using tongue-and-groove fir flooring. Fir is strong, durable, and doesn't readily warp or cup. Today, however, top-quality fir boards that are free from defects, such as knots, are increasingly rare and expensive. The tongue-and-groove boards that might serve as flooring are from softer wood

◄ Expensive—but undeniably beautiful— floors of mahogany lend rich wood tones to this grand porch added over an attached garage. Traditionally used as the decking for ocean-going ships, mahogany is naturally resistant to moisture. This floor is protected with two coats of clear polyurethane.

The ageless beauty of terra-cotta tile is apparent in the porch floor of this Italianate house built in 1802. The raised concrete porch was added years later, and provides a stable subsurface for the tile. Stability is key to tile floors: Wood subfloors should be covered with a cement-based backer board before tile is installed. And the floor should slope away from the house to shed water.

species, such as pine or hemlock, and are much more prone to warping and cupping when exposed to the elements. This type of lumber also is susceptible to rot caused by moisture trapped inside the tongue-and-groove joints. For these reasons, most builders prefer not to use tongue-and-groove boards for porch flooring. A better choice is square-edged lumber that has been treated with a wood preservative or sealer prior to installation. Over time the joints between the boards will open slightly, allowing rainwater or melted snow to drip to the ground below.

All sides of each board should be coated with a preservative that is allowed to dry for two or three days before being installed. Sealer should be applied to any freshly cut ends before they are fastened to joists. Another option is to use pressure-treated wood. This chemically treated, rot-resistant type of wood is often shipped from the factory while still moist. Bundles should be separated and the boards allowed to dry

completely before installing. The color of pressure-treated wood is dull green or brown. If you want to paint pressure-treated lumber, buy kiln-dried or wait about six months for the wood to dry completely before painting.

While a natural wood finish makes an attractive floor, a painted floor adds color and some protection against the elements. Top-quality exterior paints made specifically for floors offer an especially tough finish that resists scrapes and scratches. For added durability, allow paint to dry thoroughly, then apply two coats of exterior-grade, clear polyurethane.

Masonry Floors

Tile, stone, and brick make excellent flooring for porches. These materials are water-resistant and are classic wall and floor finishes for high-moisture areas such as bathrooms, kitchens, and mudrooms. They install readily over a concrete slab.

Tile and stone can be installed on elevated porches, although the additional structural materials required to withstand the considerable weight makes porch installation costly and rare. Refer to local building codes to determine the complexity of the substructure. For stability and to prevent cracking grout lines, a subfloor not less than 1¼ inches thick usually is required. The thickness generally is created by using sheets of ¾-inch, exterior-grade plywood covered by ½-inch-thick sheets of cementitious backer board—a material designed specifically for tile installations. As with any porch floor, creating a slope so that water runs away from the house is imperative.

Indoor-Outdoor Carpet

Indoor-outdoor carpet is designed to withstand moisture and temperature fluctuations, and it is treated to resist the fading effects of ultraviolet light associated with direct sunlight. It is available in a wide variety of styles, colors, and textures. Indoor-outdoor carpet is an excellent way to create a comfortable living area in a porch environment.

This type of carpet is glued to subfloors using a strong, water-resistant glue. Solvent-based glue generally is superior to latex-based glue because it can be applied in a wider range of weather conditions and is more water-resistant. It installs readily over concrete slabs that are dry and free from alkali residue. For porches with wood substructures, indoor-outdoor carpet requires a smooth subfloor. It can be installed over regular board flooring, but a subfloor of exterior-grade plywood is recommended. A stable plywood subfloor will help the carpet maintain its good looks for years. Waxed or oiled wood floors require resurfacing before they can be used as a subfloor for gluing down indoor-outdoor carpet.

If you decide to install indoor-outdoor carpet, consider it a permanent commitment—removing it is difficult and painstaking.

PAINT PIZAZZ

A painted floor doesn't have to just lie there; it can jump with color. Enliven your porch by creating geometric patterns with masking tape and experimenting with bold designs. The entire floor shown here was first painted with green floor paint. It was divided into a check pattern of 2-foot squares by masking off and adding white spaces. Then each white square received a dappled sponging of green paint for a mottled effect. Finally, smaller squares of black paint were added over the intersecting points of the larger squares. The whole job was protected with two coats of clear polyurethane.

Plain wood floors are easily dressed up with durable rugs of woven cotton, braided wool, or sisal. Inexpensive rugs add a dash of color and won't break the budget if they need replacing.

Walls and Screens

Porches purposely have few walls, and any existing walls or new walls should receive careful consideration to ensure they are integral to the overall design of the project. Your porch will include at least one of three types: existing exterior walls; walls made with screening material for screen porches; and low knee walls that run around the perimeter of the porch.

Existing Walls

Exterior house walls often are covered with house siding. Generally, siding makes an attractive, durable finish and emphasizes the fact that a porch is an exterior room. Because it is already installed, it's a cost-effective wall covering. There is no need to replace siding during a porch-building project unless it is in extremely poor condition, or if replacing it is part of a larger renovation project.

A new porch will put you close to at least a portion of the home's siding. Make sure it is in good repair by replacing broken or warped wood, repainting worn surfaces, and caring for masonry by replacing missing grout and patching chipped stucco. Once repaired, the walls will be protected from sun and precipitation by the porch roof and should remain in good condition for many years.

If you don't care for the appearance of your siding,

camouflage it with porch furnishings, such as shelves, and tall potted plants. Arrange seating so that it faces away from the porch walls. Add interesting details to porch posts and balustrades that draw attention away from walls. A stylish front door or a new window gives plain walls a dash of character.

▶ A total renovation of a 1908 farmhouse afforded the chance to replace old lap siding with stylish cut shingles. The soft gray of the shingles contrasts nicely with a sea-green ceiling and crisp white trim. Pillows and flowers add splashes of color.

▲ *This tastefully designed three-season porch features screen partitions with gracefully arched tops. Although this porch is not far enough off the ground to require a safety railing, a simple wooden grid adds style and prevents damage to the screen.*

Screening Options

First developed in the 1800s to keep pests out of house interiors, fine-mesh insect screen is virtually unchanged from its original design. Manufactured in several widths, it can be used for seamless panels up to 60 inches wide. Consider large openings carefully—the wider the opening, the more susceptible the screen is to sagging. Openings 42 inches wide or less are recommended. Remember that small children and pets can wreck the lower portion of screened walls, and large openings increase the cost of repairs. One solution is to build low knee walls 24 to 32 inches high between the vertical structural members. Most building codes require walls or railings 36 inches high on porches with floors more than 30 inches from the ground.

You can attach screen material directly to framing members, but a better method is to create removable screen panels. Panels should fit precisely between framing members and are held in place with clips. This way, they remove easily for repair or storage. Include storage space for screens as part of your plan.

Screen is made of either fiberglass or aluminum wire mesh, and costs about 20 cents per square foot. Fiberglass screen is lightweight, easy to work with, and won't discolor with age; however, it has a tendency to stretch and, if bumped or poked, doesn't recover its original tautness. It also tears easily. Aluminum screen is tougher than fiberglass and more capable of withstanding abuse. It resists corrosion but discolors with age. Both fiberglass and aluminum screen come in colors, usually a gray and a black or charcoal finish. The selection is a matter of visual preference—dark finishes resist glare and are good choices for sunny locations.

Another option is copper screen. It is expensive—$1.50 to $2 per square foot—but it is tougher than either fiberglass or aluminum, holding its shape against bumps and bangs. It first appears as a gleaming, coppery color and later turns a mellow brown.

Knee Walls

Some styles of houses include low walls, sometimes called knee walls, as part of the porch design. Shingle-style houses and Craftsman bungalows are two architectural types that typically have solid knee walls running along the porch perimeter, with support columns for the roof placed on solid, bearing portions of the walls.

Most building codes require porches more than 30 inches above the ground to be protected by railings that are at least 36 inches high and have balusters spaced no more than 4 inches apart—requirements satisfied by the construction of a knee wall. However, solid knee walls add considerable mass to the exterior of a home and should be carefully designed to fit its style. Usually this seamless appearance is accomplished by covering the knee wall with the same exterior siding material used on the rest of the house.

To allow moisture to drain from porch flooring, solid walls should include holes or *scuppers* at floor level. Typically, scuppers are 2 or 3 inches high, 6 to 8 inches wide, and are spaced every 6 to 8 feet around the knee wall.

▼ *Turn-of-the-century Craftsman-style houses typically have porches with solid kneewalls. This elegant beauty shows a classic finishing detail for solid porch walls—siding material and color matched to the main house.*

Ceilings

Porch ceilings are one of three types: open ceilings, revealing the supporting rafters; closed ceilings, vaulted to follow the roof pitch and with finish materials attached directly to the rafters; and drop ceilings with finish materials applied to the undersides of level, horizontal ceiling joists (see Anatomy of a Porch, pages 40–43).

Because porch ceilings are well-protected from the elements, many types of finish materials can be installed, even water-resistant drywall. Some home improvement centers carry exterior ceiling materials made of textured aluminum with a baked-on enamel finish. Use galvanized nails and exterior-grade paints, however, to combat the effects of high humidity and temperature fluctuations.

Open ceilings are the simplest and least expensive option. They are especially appropriate for rustic or country-style porches where the visible rafters add a casual, relaxed ambience. If looks are important, consider the kind of roof sheathing to use—this material is visible from below. A good grade of plywood or tongue-and-groove board makes an attractive surface. Staining rafters and sheathing a dark color helps hide imperfections.

Make sure the sheathing is thick enough to hide the tips of nails used to secure the roofing material. Use ¾-inch-thick sheathing and roofing nails no longer than ¾ inch to ensure the nails remain hidden. Camouflage framing lumber by staining or painting the entire ceiling a uniform color.

Closed ceilings present a flat, uniform surface when viewed from below. The finish material can be almost anything that can withstand the elements. Add a bit of texture with tongue-and-groove boards or with decorative plywood that features the classic finishing detail for porch ceilings—beaded board. Remember that plywood sheets create seams where the sheets butt each

> *Exposed rafters and roof sheathing add touches of rustic comfort to this spacious, multi-sided porch addition. Because the sheathing would be visible from below, the owners chose the look of individual boards, rather than sheets of plywood, that emphasize the structure's shape.*

other. Plan to cover seams with battens installed at regular intervals along the rafters.

Closed ceilings have an advantage over open ceilings because electrical wiring and cables are concealed between the roof sheathing and the ceiling finish. This makes installing lighting fixtures and ceiling fans a more visually attractive option.

Drop ceilings give porches a cozy, roomlike feel. Because ceilings are a prominent feature of porch design, the finish material should be top-quality.

Both tongue-and-groove boards and decorative plywood make attractive surfaces. For tongue-and-groove boards, stagger end seams throughout the ceiling. Cover plywood butt joints with battens. If you plan to install a ceiling fan, allow a clearance of at least 7 feet between the floor and the fan blades. To keep hanging switch chains from becoming an annoyance, operate fans and lights from a wall-mounted switch.

When this backyard screen porch was renovated, most of the woodwork received a fresh coat of paint. The original beaded board ceiling, however, has the priceless dark patina of age that the owners preserved.

▲ *This 1970s suburban house was just plain typical before it was reenergized with a big, friendly porch. A front-facing gable placed directly over the doorway and stairway indicates the home's primary entry.*

Doors and Entryways

Classic porch style aligns the front stairs with the main doorway. This language of house-building makes it clear to visitors where they are to approach and enter a home. It also is the most efficient use of porch space, creating the shortest possible route from stairway to entry door and reserving the remainder of the porch area as living space. A centrally placed entry door bisects a large porch into two areas, establishing two separate outdoor living spaces. If you are planning a porch project and have the option of placing a front door in a number of locations, consider how you will use your porch. Placing the stairs and entry off to one side allows for one large area for entertaining friends and family.

Stairs that lead directly to a front door are one way to clearly establish the preferred place of entry. Others include painting the door a color that stands apart from the surrounding color scheme. You don't have to select a brash hue to create this effect—

ACCESSIBLE STAIRWAY

Accommodating people with special needs requires sensitive—and imaginative—solutions. This is especially true of wheelchair ramps, which may have considerable length. The architect for the historic house shown on this page had even more considerations—his final design had to meet the approval of the local historical commission. The answer is a broad porch that houses a wheelchair ramp. Because the ramp flows side-to-side, the depth of the porch is in keeping with the architectural style of the house. Across the front, level railings and a curb wall present the illusion of a typical elevated porch deck.

Although looks may be important, the practical concerns of creating an accessible, easy-to-use ramp are primary considerations. The basic principles of ramp design specify a slope of 1 vertical inch for every 12 inches of run for unassisted (hand-operated) wheelchair use. A doorway located 30 inches above grade would require a wheelchair ramp 30 feet long for unassisted use. If the ramp is to be used exclusively by persons with assisted (motorized) wheelchairs, a slope of 2 vertical inches for every 12 inches of run is allowed. Landings in front of doors should be at least 36 inches wide and 60 inches deep for in-swinging doors, and 60 inches square for out-swinging doors.

a solid block of contrasting color will suffice. Moldings, such as pilasters and pediments, are classic design motifs that have been used for centuries to emphasize entry doors. Another effective technique is to create a small, front-facing gable roof over the entry steps.

Large porches and wraparound designs offer the possibility of adding a second entry door. Plan second entryways carefully—they should be integrated with the interior design and configuration of your home. A door that opens into your living or dining room will no doubt get extra use from active kids and pets with muddy feet. A better choice is to allow access to a kitchen or to create a private entry for a bedroom or home office. While you emphasize the location of your main entry, you'll probably want to de-emphasize the second, more secluded entry. Keep moldings and paint colors subtle. Remember that stairways leading directly to doors act as open invitations to approach.

Stairs and Railings

Stairways are one of the most important elements of a porch. They must be safe, sturdy, and good-looking. Because they project outward, they are a dramatic visual element that commands attention. During planning, give your stairway careful consideration to ensure it is a graceful and welcoming part of the overall design.

Railings are a primary safety feature of raised decks, platforms, or porches, and they are a basic feature of stairways. Typically, the design of the railing system is mirrored in the balustrade of the stairway. A porch railing system includes handrails, balusters, and posts. These parts can be made of wood, high-density urethane and molded polymers, or wood covered with vinyl.

Wood offers strength and crisp, well-defined details. Although wooden porch parts typically are made from rot-resistant redwood or cedar, they require periodic maintenance with top-quality exterior-grade paint or stain. You'll find a large variety of shapes and styles from companies that specialize in wooden parts.

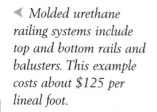

◄ *Molded urethane railing systems include top and bottom rails and balusters. This example costs about $125 per lineal foot.*

▲ *The porch of this turn-of-the-century cottage was a comfortable space but the roof was supported by skinny metal posts and there were no railings. The homeowners gave the porch a facelift by adding fluted columns and a nicely detailed railing system made of molded polymer. Because polymer moldings are paintable, trim colors were added to match the paint scheme of the house.*

▶ This 12-inch-square newel post is made of polyurethane and features a structural steel core. It costs about $300.

Parts made from high-density urethane and molded polymers are virtually weather- and rot-proof and require little maintenance. They usually come from the factory with a baked-on white primer that can stand as the finish coat, or they can be painted. They are structurally sound and meet or exceed building code requirements. These parts are made as systems that fit together with little measuring or cutting. Because they are produced in molds, there is some sacrifice in the sharpness of detail they provide.

Wooden parts covered with vinyl are the least expensive and typically are available in home improvement centers. The wooden core is made with pressure-treated wood that provides strength and resistance to rot, and the vinyl coverings are maintenance-free. They come in standard sizes and may have to be adjusted on-site to fit individual porches.

◀ With motifs inspired by Victorian farmhouses of the late 19th century, this newly built home in Colorado shows how a porch can be carefully integrated into the overall design. A simple railing, posts, and stairs are all that's needed to make a grand entryway.

One challenging element of designing good-looking railings and stairs is creating even spacing between porch posts. The design must take into account the placement of stairs with regard to the main entry door, the number of supporting posts required to hold up the porch roof, and the overall length of the porch deck. Juggling these numbers and ending up with a pleasing design is no simple task. One solution is to adjust the overall size of the porch to facilitate even spacings. Another is to adjust the placement of one or more posts to produce differences in spacings that are virtually undetectable.

Include the landing at the bottom of the stairs in your plans. This area should be integral to the overall design of the stairway. A patio or walkway made of brick, concrete, or stone forms the ideal approach to stairs. Plan the surrounding landscaping as a visual complement.

▶ *Porch railings typically span between a column that supports the roof and a railing post. All supports must be taken into account when planning a railing layout. This finely detailed example features fanciful post caps.*

CODE REQUIREMENTS FOR STAIRS AND RAILINGS

The design of stairs and railings is strictly regulated by building codes. Although codes vary from region to region, most include these basic requirements:
- Raised floor surfaces (decks) located more than 30 inches above grade (ground) must have guardrails at least 36 inches high.
- Stairs more than 30 inches high must have guardrails at least 34 inches high, measured from the nosing of the stairs.
- Guardrails must have intermediate rails or posts or other ornamental fill that will not pass an object 4 inches in diameter (a 4-inch ball).
- The height of stair handrails must be between 30 and 38 inches, measured directly above the nosing of the tread.
- There must be a handrail on at least one side of a stairway that has more than two risers.
- The minimum distance for treads, measured nose-to-nose, is 10 inches.
- The maximum height of a riser is 7¾ inches. (Note: A riser 6 inches high and a tread 12 inches deep are recommended for outdoor stairways.)
- The dimensions of treads and risers cannot vary by more than ⅜ inch from step to step.

▶ *This turned redwood post is 8 feet tall and costs about $300.*

Decorative Details

Most porches include some kind of detailing. Decorative brackets, moldings that encircle posts, and trim that enhances roof fascia are examples of details that give a porch personality and character. Porch detailing usually derives from architectural details that are copied from other parts of the house, such as brackets under an eave or moldings used to trim a dormer window. Use these visual clues as a key to selecting details that are properly scaled, visually appealing, and well-matched to the style of your house.

Some styles of house use many applied details. Victorian houses are well-known for their use of

▲ Decorative wood brackets characterize houses made in the Victorian style. Like many Victorian details, these brackets have a multicolor paint scheme that requires regular maintenance and touch-up.

▲ Not all detailing is elaborate. This simple flat railing made of ¾-inch paint-grade pine protects the screen of this three-season porch from accidental bumps and pokes.

> *Remodelings and additions over its almost 200-year history gave this Federal-style house elements from other eras. The fanciful porch was probably added in the late 19th century. Small brackets under the eaves, fluted columns, and arched openings identify the Italianate style.*

complex ornamentation, often called gingerbread. There are so many individual pieces to Victorian detailing that a unique vocabulary was developed to identify each component: Fan brackets, scrollwork spandrels, beaded rails, and medallions are just a few of the decorative components of a Victorian porch. Although beautiful, remember that detailed trim can be expensive. If your porch project is for a Victorian house, study the possibilities carefully and compose a complete materials list before making the final decision. An architect or other professional designer can help you make choices that are in keeping with the style of your home and that won't break your project budget.

For most other houses, moderation is always a good guideline—a little bit of ornamentation can go a long way. Try simple brackets and modest trims that provide graceful accents and won't overwhelm the overall appearance of the porch. Remember

> *Crown molding made of urethane would be installed under the eaves of a classically styled porch.*

Decorative brackets on older homes were often custom-designed by the builder and made on-site.
Ornate moldings and paint schemes characterize Victorian porch designs. The small white blocks are dentils.

that paint also can act as a decorative detail, creating interesting lines and contrasts that are attractive and less expensive than applied moldings and trims.

As with other porch components, decorative details are made from wood and urethane or molded polymers. Wood details are available in an enormous variety of styles and sizes, and they can be custom-made to match existing details—an important consideration if you own a historic house. They usually are made from rot-resistant redwood or cedar and will require periodic maintenance with top-quality exterior-grade paint or stain.

Details made of molded polymers or urethane are durable, weatherproof, and don't rot. They can be painted to coordinate with the house colors or left with the factory white finish. They are attached like wood components—with galvanized nails or screws. They tend to be more expensive than wood parts of similar size and shape but compensate by requiring less maintenance.

Elements of Style
Sunrooms

Becoming familiar with
surfaces and materials.

The definition of the word *sunroom* is a bit inexact. The term simply refers to an area of the home with an abundance of windows oriented to receive a maximum amount of sun. The classic example of a sunroom is a conservatory, a space made mostly of glass—including the ceiling. Other versions include one-story rooms featuring plenty of windows, glass doors, and skylights. A third style has windows or glass doors but no overhead glazing, characteristically a sunroom on the first floor of a two-story home.

Sunrooms are similar to porches because they are often used as transition spaces between the indoor and outdoor environments. In good weather, screened sunroom windows and doors can open to breezes, creating a room similar to a screen porch. Hard-surface, water-resistant flooring, such as tile or stone, is common in sunrooms because these spaces often are used for growing plants in all seasons and must endure occasional spills. Sunrooms include heating systems that keep them warm all year—walls, ceilings, and floors must be completely insulated.

You'll find two basic options in sunroom construction: One is to build an addition or add a prefabricated model. This requires determining the proper orientation for your sunroom in regard to the movement of the sun. Also, you must find a satisfactory place to attach the sunroom to your house so that the addition is a logical extension of your living area. Most likely, you will need to knock out an existing wall or, at the least, create a doorway to your sunroom.

The other option is to turn an existing room into a sunroom by replacing solid exterior walls with windows or glass doors, and adding skylights. Again, proper orientation to the sun's position throughout the year is a key factor for capturing maximum sunlight and making your sunroom the bright, cheerful place you envision.

In either case, choosing proper windows and doors is an important part of your plan. Familiarize yourself with the many types of glazings and configurations available so that your sunroom is well designed for your region of the country and your particular needs.

▼ Outfitting a south-facing exterior wall with a bank of large insulated-glass windows turned the living room of this ranch house into a bright sunroom. A pair of old French doors with leaded glass, found at an architectural salvage shop, adds style.

▲ *Adding a sunroom to a suburban house created a generous dining area for a growing family. The addition sits at grade level on a concrete slab that extends to form walkways and a surrounding patio.*

Anatomy of a Sunroom

The design of the sunroom and the configuration of the large amounts of windows, glass doors, and skylights are a matter of personal preference. Other than that, a sunroom is built using conventional construction techniques and methods. It's a good idea to have a basic understanding of sunroom construction and terminology so that you're able to communicate effectively with an architect, a building contractor, and other professionals involved in the design and construction of your sunroom.

Foundations

A sunroom must have a concrete foundation that complies with local building codes. The foundation footings must be deeper than the frost line, typically a distance of 36 to 48 inches below grade. This prevents the foundation from moving when the soil expands and contracts as it freezes during colder months.

If it is possible to build on grade, consider a slab foundation. A slab foundation works especially well as the base for tile or stone flooring—both popular choices for sunroom floors. It also is appropriate for vinyl, carpet, plastic laminate, and many types of

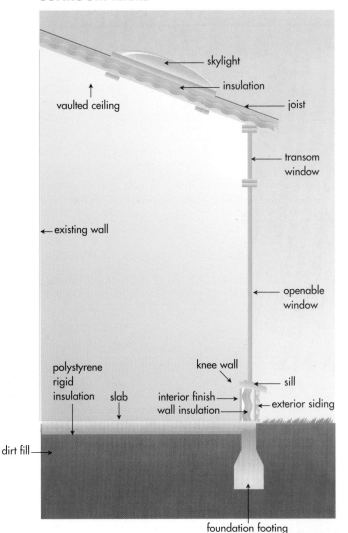

vaulted ceiling

skylight

insulation

joist

transom window

existing wall

openable window

polystyrene rigid insulation

slab

knee wall

sill

interior finish wall insulation

exterior siding

dirt fill

foundation footing

glue-down wood flooring (see Flooring, pages 75–81). If growing plants is an important part of your plan and your sunroom will be exposed to frequent waterings and occasional spills, consider sloping a slab floor toward a centrally located drain. A drain system requires careful planning so that the drain pipe can be tied to your existing main drain or septic system. Consulting a qualified plumber will be an essential part of your design process.

A slab floor also presents an interesting heating option. Fitted with a radiant heat system, a slab floor offers one of the most comfortable types of home heating available. Radiant heating systems are expensive (see Heating and Cooling, pages 65–69). Consult with a licensed heating and cooling contractor about installing a radiant heat system in your slab floor.

If your sunroom is not directly on grade, you'll build a conventionally framed foundation consisting of concrete footings that comply with local building codes; exterior foundation walls of concrete, cement block, or wood; a framing system of girders and joists; and a subfloor. Conventionally built foundations are fairly inexpensive and straightforward to construct. The space underneath the flooring system is called the crawlspace. It is convenient for adding heating and cooling ductwork, electrical cables, and even plumbing pipes.

◄ *A prefabricated sunroom is a simple addition project. This glass-roofed version was tucked under an eave and forms a small courtyard. Even small prefabricated sunrooms must rest on a foundation that complies with local building codes.*

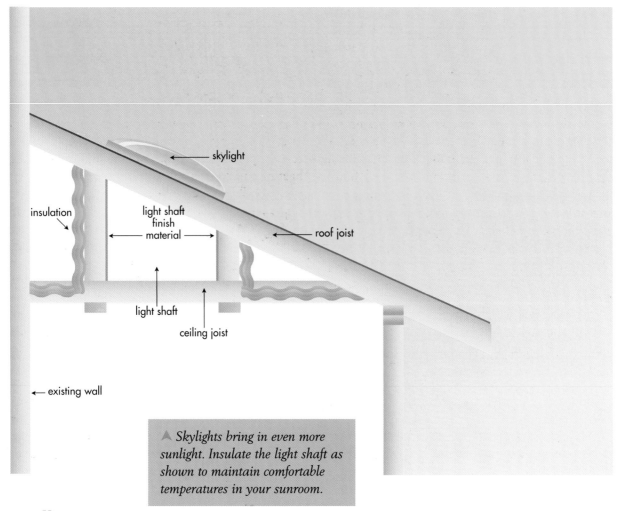

insulation

skylight

light shaft finish material

roof joist

light shaft

ceiling joist

existing wall

▲ *Skylights bring in even more sunlight. Insulate the light shaft as shown to maintain comfortable temperatures in your sunroom.*

Walls

Sunroom walls are framed conventionally—with wood studs. To maximize the insulating power of your walls, specify 2×6 studs for more space for insulation, or use a higher R-value insulation in standard 2×4 walls. However, most of your sunroom walls will be glass—either windows or doors. Selecting high-performance glazing is one of the most important choices for your sunroom (see Windows, Doors, and Skylights, pages 70–74). Glazing should be designed to gather the most sunlight when you want it, prevent sunlight from entering the sunroom when you don't, and retain heat during winter months, especially at night.

Roofs

With the exception of all-glass conservatories or prefabricated sunspaces, sunroom roofs are framed conventionally, using joists of appropriate size and spacing. Design roofs with as much insulation as possible so that during colder months the sunroom retains as much heat as possible.

The number and size of skylight openings is a matter of personal preference. Control the amount of sunlight by specifying skylights fitted with operable shades or blinds. Most skylight manufacturers offer units with many shading options and insulating capabilities.

Overhead glazings must meet requirements for safety specified by local building codes. Typically, safety glass is tempered, is laminated with a plastic layer, or features wire imbedded in the glass. Standard skylights and roof windows already meet strict specifications for overhead glazing safety.

Heating and Cooling

Proper heating and cooling are essential for comfort in a sunroom where large expanses of glazing cause rapid heat gain and loss. Your sunroom should employ both active and passive techniques for controlling temperature fluctuations. Active techniques use mechanical systems for heating and cooling. Passive techniques use shading and ventilation to control sunlight and encourage air circulation.

Extending an Existing Mechanical System

If your sunroom addition is fairly modest—about 400 square feet or less—controlling the temperature is typically a matter of extending the existing heating and cooling system. Although your existing system will be sized for your present house, it probably can handle this small additional load. A larger room may require a supplemental heating and cooling unit or retrofitting your current system. A heating contractor or mechanical engineer can advise you about the feasibility of extending your present system.

To extend a forced-air system, you must add a supplemental duct to the main duct. A forced-air system also requires air-return ducts. New ducts should be properly sized for the addition, and should meet all building code requirements for length and the number of turns allowed along the

◄ *An all-glass roof lets in abundant daylight and requires a system to control glare and prevent excessive heat gain. The owners of this bright San Diego sunroom hung white muslin swags over the steel collar ties to provide shade and offer a bit of South Seas romance.*

length. Air ducts are fairly large (typically 5–6 inches in diameter for round pipe and 2×12 inches for rectangular) and it is often difficult to find unrestricted routes for new ducts without tearing out portions of existing walls or ceilings. Be prepared for the added expense of renovation work to accommodate new ducts. Hot-water heating systems are easier to extend because water pipe has a small diameter (typically ½ or ¾ inches) that allows it to be easily run through joists or into existing walls.

Mechanically controlling the temperature is another consideration. If you have one centrally located thermostat, it probably means your home is set up as a single zone. A sunroom addition, with its tendency toward large temperature fluctuations, could have very different temperature requirements than other areas. What your lone thermostat

▲ *Surrounded by deciduous trees—those that lose their leaves in the fall—this cozy sunroom is well shaded from summer's hottest sun. When fall arrives, sunlight helps warm the interior.*

determines is correct for the majority of your house may not be appropriate for the sunroom. Establish a second, thermostatically controlled zone to ensure comfortable temperatures for your sunroom. Again, consult a mechanical engineer or heating contractor about creating a second thermostatically controlled zone.

Supplemental Heating and Cooling

There are many small, lightweight heating and cooling appliances that are relatively easy to add to a new sunroom. Each has a built-in thermostat and temperature-control settings. Be aware that these appliances make considerable demands on your home's electrical system. It is a good idea to consult with a heating and cooling expert or a licensed electrician about whether your supplemental heater or air-conditioner needs to be placed on its own electrical circuit.

• *Baseboard heaters* come in lengths of 4 or 6 feet, use normal household electrical current, and can be plugged into a wall outlet or hard-wired to an electrical circuit. Baseboard heaters are quiet, efficient, and generally easy to conceal.

• *Electric wall heaters* have built-in fans to distribute heat and are small enough to be inconspicuous. They install between studs and are covered with a grill or faceplate that extends about ¾ inch beyond the wall surface. Wall heaters use standard household current but must be hard-wired into your home's electrical circuits.

• *Portable air-conditioners*, sometimes called window air-conditioners, are good at providing supplemental cooling. Before purchasing a window unit, determine the square footage of the sunroom addition. Window units usually are rated by the square footage they can effectively cool. Place these units in a window or in a wall opening created just for them so they won't obstruct daylight or views. Although they are more noticeable when placed high on a wall, this location provides the best distribution of cool air.

• *Ductless heat pumps* are used for both heating and cooling. They have two major components—an indoor air handler and an outdoor compressor. They are connected to each other by a refrigerant-carrying line that can be up to 160 feet long. Because the refrigerant line requires a hole no larger than 3 inches in diameter, ductless heat pumps are ideal for conversion projects that require supplemental heating and cooling or as an independent source of heating and cooling for rooms isolated on their own thermostat.

• *Gas fireplaces*, also called direct-vent fireplaces, add heat and ambience. They are rated by the size of the room they effectively heat. Be sure to find the right one for your particular room size. They require a natural gas line and a location for a vent—usually a 3-inch diameter pipe with an inner chamber for exhaust gases and an outer sleeve that pulls in outside air for combustion. Some types of direct-vent heaters can be thermostatically controlled. Most units are stylishly designed to fit with a variety of interior designs.

▷ *Pleated cellular blinds set between the window frames help soften harsh sunlight. Drawing the blinds from bottom to top allows them to be positioned for privacy.*

• *Ceiling fans* don't control temperature, but they promote air circulation and make rooms feel comfortably cool. Ceiling fans come in an array of styles, shapes, and sizes to fit any decor. You can install a ceiling fan in your sunroom ceiling as long as you have enough headroom. Most building codes specify a distance of not less than 80 inches from the bottom of the ceiling fan to the finished floor. Remember that this distance should be measured from the lowest part of the fan—typically the lighting fixture.

Passive Techniques for Heating and Cooling

Glassed-in sunrooms are designed to gather daylight—usually as much as possible. As a building material, glass has unique characteristics that bear on the design of sunrooms. Basically, glass permits light to pass through but doesn't let it back out. When light energy strikes solid objects, such as walls, floors, and furniture, it immediately changes into heat in a process known as heat gain. Although glass is not a great insulator, it does inhibit heat from leaving interior spaces, thus trapping the sun's heat.

Today's glass and window manufacturers have overcome the shortcomings of glass and have created products that have excellent clarity yet prevent the transfer of heat—such as double-insulating windows that are the standard of the industry. This type of glazing allows sunlight through and retains heat for long periods (see Windows, Doors, and Skylights, pages 70–74).

Shades and other passive techniques for controlling sunlight and heat gain are the most important factors in creating comfortable sunroom living areas. They also help reduce the cost of operating mechanical systems that heat and cool a sunroom. Passive techniques are influenced by the seasons. In the summer, keep sunlight out during the hottest portions of the day. In winter, invite sunlight in to maximize heat gain. Spring and fall are more challenging—what begins as a chilly day can quickly turn quite warm, requiring a bit of work on the homeowner's part to establish the correct combination of passive techniques to create and maintain comfortable temperatures.

The easiest way to control sunlight is with shades, curtains, or blinds. The choice is a matter of personal preference and is often determined by the interior design of the space. Some blinds include reflective material that bounce sunlight back through windows before it has a chance to turn into heat. Some windows and doors feature built-in blinds—the blinds are in the dead-air space between the panes of insulating glass. These types of blinds are easily controlled, allow other decorative window treatments to be installed, and never need cleaning. Manufacturers of skylights also offer many types of built-in shading options for their products, including roller shades, pleated blinds, and horizontal blinds.

The eaves that overhang your sunroom are another way to control unwanted heat gain. In the summer, eaves shade vertical windows during the

hottest part of the day—when the sun is directly overhead. During winter, however, when the sun is lower on the horizon, eaves will not block sunlight, permitting maximum heat gain.

Another good passive strategy is to locate a sunroom so that deciduous trees—those that lose their leaves in fall—will shade the sunroom during summer, *right*. During winter, when the leaves are gone, deciduous trees will allow sunlight to warm sunroom spaces.

Natural Ventilation

Use natural convection to keep air circulating through a sunroom when weather is warm or temperate. Natural convection takes advantage of a simple principle—hot air rises. By establishing vents or window openings at low and high points within a sunroom, natural convection is used to exhaust hot, stagnant air through upper openings while introducing cooler air through lower openings. The higher your ceiling, the better this principle will work. Vaulted ceilings work best because they channel hot air toward the highest point in the room.

Use a combination of windows and skylights to establish natural convection air currents, *right*. Ideally, have a row of small windows, or the lower portions of double-hung windows, serve as air intakes and a skylight to permit warm, rising air to escape. If temperature control is important (for example, if you are growing plants and need to ensure that temperatures don't get too high), consider installing a thermostatically controlled exhaust fan in the upper portion of a wall. When temperatures rise, the thermostat automatically turns on the fan, even when the household cooling system is off.

Radiant Heating

Radiant heating systems are increasingly popular because they warm the floor—not just the air circulating within a room—so that heat is delivered directly to the body's lower extremities. The result is a greater sense of warmth and comfort. Thermostats can be set to lower temperatures than with forced-air systems, thus reducing heating costs. Also, radiant systems don't require mechanical openings, such as ventilation grates, meaning greater flexibility with interior design schemes.

There are two types of radiant heating systems. Hydronic systems use tough, flexible polyethylene tubing to carry hot water through circulating coils and loops that heat floors. The tubes can be fastened to the underside of the subfloor between joists, embedded in a concrete slab, or placed on top of a conventional wood floor system and covered

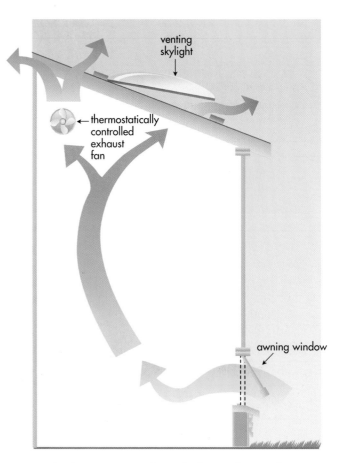

▲ *Cool air comes in through the window at the bottom and is drawn up as warm air exits through the skylight. An exhaust fan and additional vents can be added to improve air circulation.*

with a layer of lightweight concrete—an installation that requires substantial structural support to carry the weight. Hot water is furnished by a boiler or water heater that is devoted to the floor heating system. Water flow and temperature are regulated by thermostatically controlled manifolds that link the runs of tubing to the heating source. Technological advances in tubing design make hydronic systems extremely reliable, and most manufacturers offer long-term guarantees against leaks or other failures.

Electrical radiant heating systems employ networks of heating cables or wires embedded in thin mats. The heating elements are protected from damage by layers of insulation and tough outer jackets made of metal or plastic. As with hydronic installations, the cables or mats may be installed underneath the subfloor, embedded in a slab, or buried in mortar. Some heating mats are designed to be installed directly under tile or stone.

Radiant heating systems installed in concrete allow the concrete to act as a thermal mass, a substance that absorbs and stores heat and releases it slowly over a period of time. The result is even, quiet distribution of heat without temperature peaks and valleys associated with forced-air systems. Concrete floors are readily covered with tile, brick, or stone—classic sunroom flooring materials that increase the amount of thermal mass available. If radiant heating is attached to the underside of a wood subfloor, the space below the heating elements is filled with insulation to ensure the heat migrates upward. Some systems include aluminum panels underneath the heating elements to reflect heat toward the living spaces.

Because the initial installation work is more time-consuming, the cost of a radiant heat system is about twice the cost of a forced-air system used to heat spaces of similar size and volume. Also, ductwork used to supply hot air for a forced-air system can be used to supply cooling; a radiant heating system must be accompanied by a supplemental cooling system. Over time, however, radiant heating costs less to operate, reducing heating expenses. Also, radiant heating systems designed with modular, easy-to-install components, along with an increasing familiarity on the part of heating and cooling contractors with these types of systems, should help lower prices in the next few years. If you are interested in radiant heating, ask your heating and cooling contractor to prepare comparative bids for the two types of systems.

▲ Radiant heating systems can be installed three ways: 1) under an existing plywood floor; 2) in concrete on top of an existing plywood floor; and 3) on top of an existing slab.

▼ *This 12×12-foot sunroom features a roof of inexpensive PVC panels screwed onto joists made from painted, pressure-treated lumber. The screen walls are fitted with plastic panels that are easily removed in warm weather.*

Windows, Doors, and Skylights

Glass windows and doors are primary components of any sunroom. The sizes and shapes offered by most window manufacturers are virtually unlimited and permit many possible configurations. Ideally, select windows that are compatible with windows you already have. For example, if your house has windows with wood grilles, you will probably want to specify grilles for the new windows installed in your sunroom. Sunrooms encourage interaction with the outdoors, and doors should be an integral part of planning.

Opening windows can turn your sunroom into a screen porch that lets in plenty of fresh air and cooling breezes. However, windows are a major expense. To conserve costs, combine less-expensive fixed windows with windows that open, and use stock rather than custom sizes.

Windows and doors are made of all-wood, vinyl, aluminum, or wood clad with vinyl or aluminum. Each of these types offers advantages in terms of energy efficiency, maintenance, and cost.

• *Wood* windows and doors are energy-efficient and widely available at home improvement centers. All-wood windows typically are the most expensive type of windows. Manufacturers of wood products usually offer some custom-capabilities for making

▶ *Positioned to take advantage of spectacular views, a sunroom dining area has subtle furnishings that underscore the drama beyond the glass wall. The upper transom windows open for ventilation.*

unusual shape windows or doors. All-wood units require periodic refinishing.

• *Vinyl* offers superior energy efficiency and moderate cost. Vinyl units are available in a few stock colors and some custom colors that are maintenance-free. They also can be painted.

• *Aluminum* windows and doors also are maintenance-free, but they are not as energy efficient as most other products. Aluminum windows and doors should include a thermal break—a material inserted into the aluminum frames to slow the transfer of heat.

• *Clad* windows and doors combine the energy-efficiency of wood frames with maintenance-free coverings of vinyl or aluminum; they also are moderately priced. Clad units are the most popular style of window and door.

Glazing Options

Most manufacturers offer options for the type of glass used for their windows and doors. The industry standard is hermetically sealed, double-pane glass with an insulating dead-air space between the panes. This type of glazing has moderate insulating capabilities and good clarity—it transmits about 85 percent of available visible light. Standard insulating glass is a good choice for most regions of the country. High-performance glazings are available to increase energy efficiency in more severe climates. Be prepared to pay a premium price for windows and doors with specialty glazings.

• *Triple-pane* glazings include three panes of glass to create two insulating spaces for added resistance to heat loss.

• *Argon-filled* windows and doors use argon gas instead of air in the space between panes of glass. Argon is an odorless, colorless, nontoxic gas with a thermal conductivity about 30 percent lower than regular air.

• *Low-emissivity* glass, usually called low-E glass, is coated with microscopically thin layers of silver and metal oxides. It permits light to pass through the glass but helps prevent heat transfer, resulting in better heat retention in the winter and decreased heat gain from outside air in the summer. Low-E glass also blocks infrared light and most ultraviolet light—the kind of light that causes fabrics to fade—but allows about 75 percent of visible light to pass.

• *Sun glazings* are specially designed to block much of the visible spectrum, thus preventing heat gain. These types of glazings are popular in the Southwest, where days are frequently sunny and hot. Sun glazings feature reflective coatings that permit only about 40 percent of visible light to reach interiors.

• *Safety glass* is required by most building codes for skylights, large glass doors, windows within 18 inches of a floor, and windows installed on walls that incline 15 degrees or more. Safety glass is either tempered, laminated, or wire glass. Tempered glass has been specially heat treated. When it breaks, it crumbles into small bits rather than large, sharp shards. Many manufacturers offer tempered safety glass as an option for their windows and doors. Laminated glass has a layer of plastic film sandwiched between two layers of glass to prevent fragments from flying if the glass is broken. Wire glass is laminated with thin wires inside. If it is struck and broken, the wires prevent hands and feet from going completely through the opening.

Skylights and Roof Windows

Skylights provide an extraordinary amount of light. Because they open toward the sky, they admit 35 to 85 percent more light than vertical windows of

◄ *Skylights with built-in shades add daylight to this sunroom in a heavily treed backyard. Canvas awnings protect west-facing windows from intense summer sun at the end of the day.*

> ▲ *To create the ambience of a canopy of trees, the owners of this spacious conservatory covered inside surfaces with stained-green lattice. The grids also help disguise the ordinary view.*

similar size. They also allow considerable solar heat gain. To prevent sunrooms from getting too hot, equip skylights with shades or blinds. Most skylight manufacturers offer many options for shading, including pleated blinds, roller blinds, and horizontal blinds. The shading material can be either translucent or opaque. Shades that are electronically operated by a wall-mounted switch are another option, allowing you to control the amount of sunlight at the touch of a button.

Skylight glazing options are similar to those of windows. Insulating glass is the industry standard. You can also specify low-E coatings, tints for reducing sunlight, and tempered safety glass.

There are three types of skylights:

• *Fixed skylights* cannot be opened and are usually the most economical units. Bubble-type skylights feature insulated dome-shaped Plexiglas that helps shed water.

• *Fixed, vented skylights* include a small vent that can be opened and closed to allow air to circulate. These types of units are less expensive than skylights that open fully.

• *Vented skylights* open with a hand crank, control rods, or electronic controls. Vented skylights are an excellent way to allow fresh air to circulate through

ENERGY EFFICIENCY

The National Fenestration Rating Council (NFRC) is an independent, nonprofit testing organization created by the window, door, and skylight industry to create standards of energy efficiency that can be applied to all windows (fenestration refers to any opening in a building, and usually means windows, doors, and skylights). Participation in the program is voluntary, and currently about 150 manufacturers allow the NFRC to rate their products.

The NFRC does not set minimum standards of performance or draw conclusions about quality and reliability. It does, however, create a simple labeling system that allows shoppers to easily compare windows and doors in regard to thermal performance. The NFRC tests three criteria:

• U-factor, or how well a window keeps heat inside a home. The lower the U-factor, the more energy-efficient the window.

• Solar heat gain, or a window's ability to block warming caused by sunlight. The higher the rating, the better the window performs at stopping solar heat gain.

• Visible light transmittance, or the clarity of a window. The higher the rating, the more light is admitted into a house.

Another well-known indicator of energy efficiency is the R-value. R-values measure a building material's resistance to heat transfer. Materials with high R-values are better insulators than those with low R-values. Most manufacturers apply this measurement to glass, although the NFRC does not offer R-value ratings.

sunrooms. Make sure a vented skylight is equipped with an insect screen to keep out pests.

Roof windows are similar to skylights. The distinction is a matter of accessibility—skylights cannot be reached while standing on the floor, but roof windows can. Both types of units can be installed on sloped roof surfaces. Flat roofs typically require a skylight to be installed on a curb wall that is designed to prevent water from entering the opening.

Flooring

Choose the type of flooring for your sunroom based on how you intend to use the space and what your budget allows. Some choices are better than others for durability, resistance to moisture, and ability to withstand the effects of ultraviolet light from direct sunlight. Masonry floors of tile, brick, and stone are classic flooring materials for sunrooms.

Ceramic Tile

Few building materials are as captivating and intriguing as ceramic tile. Ceramic flooring tile is readily available in varieties appropriate to almost all architectural styles and eras.

Generally, floor tiles are harder and more durable than tiles made for walls or countertops. In addition, floor tiles have different degrees of resistance to abrasion, slippage, staining, and breakage. An abrasion-resistant tile is recommended for areas that have high traffic, such as entryways, or for dining rooms, where chairs are constantly moved back and forth. Where abrasion is minimal, a nonporous, slip-resistant tile is preferred. When selecting tiles for floors, always check the manufacturer's recommendation.

The American National Standards Institute (ANSI) has developed ratings that help determine the proper tile to use in various settings. ANSI has established four categories that define tiles by their ability to absorb water, or porosity. Generally, these categories reflect how a tile is manufactured. Tiles made with lower temperatures and shorter kiln times tend to be softer and more porous, making the tile more susceptible to staining or breakage. Tiles fired

◄ *Earthy tumbled marble, set in a checkerboard pattern of light and dark colors, creates a classic—and classy—sunroom floor. While resistant to moisture, most natural stone products must be sealed to prevent staining.*

> *Adding a perimeter foundation to support the walls and a roof turned this former patio into a sunny three-season porch. The original weathered patio brick remains as a rustic and durable floor.*

at higher temperatures and for longer periods are hard and dense, and more resistant to abrasion and stains.

• *Impervious*—absorbs less than 0.5 percent of its weight in water. These tiles can stand heavy traffic and very wet conditions, including areas that often have standing water. They withstand freezing and are ideal for all-weather outdoor use.

• *Vitreous*—absorbs more than 0.5 percent and less than 3 percent. A vitreous tile is a good all-around indoor flooring choice and is suitable for bathrooms, kitchens, and sunrooms.

• *Semivitreous*—absorbs more than 3 percent and less than 7 percent. Because a semivitreous tile may be prone to staining, it may require sealing before it can be used in wet areas. Be sure to check the manufacturer's recommendation.

• *Nonvitreous*—absorbs more than 7 percent. Usually not recommended for floors.

Floor tiles are either glazed or unglazed. Both types can be used for flooring, and the difference between the two types is usually a matter of color.

Unglazed tiles characteristically take their earthy colors from the color of the fired clay. Glazed tiles have a colored ceramic coating that is bonded to the tile in a kiln at temperatures up to 2,300 degrees. Glazing can help tiles resist stains and moisture, but check to see if the manufacturer has provided a hardness rating for the glazing that will help you determine whether it is a good choice as a flooring material. A rating of 5 or 6 is appropriate for low-traffic areas, and higher ratings indicate the tile is a good choice for most flooring installations. There are four basic tile choices:

• *Quarry tile* is a tough, durable tile ideal for flooring. Made of a mixture of clay and shale that is fired at high temperatures, quarry tile is usually unglazed and is available in a variety of natural earth tones such as brown, dark red, yellow, and gray. Slight variations in the color of each tile give each floor unique characteristics. Quarry tile has a slightly textured, skid-resistant surface. It is stain-resistant, but most manufacturers recommend sealing quarry tile to prevent discoloration.

• *Terra-cotta* often refers to the look of a tile rather than specific properties or process of manufacture. Generally, terra-cotta tiles are thought of as being rustic, handmade tiles imported from Mexico or Europe with uneven edges, pitting, and other surface imperfections that give them distinctive character. Today, however, they also can be purchased with smooth, even surfaces and well-defined edges. Terra-cotta tiles are usually unglazed and have the same natural clay colors—ocher and umber—as quarry tile. Due to the many different techniques used to produce terra-cotta tiles, they will vary in price and quality. Most are rated as semivitreous. Always check the manufacturer's recommendations before specifying terra-cotta tiles.

• *Porcelain* floor tiles are made at very high temperatures that make them extremely hard and stain-resistant and an excellent choice for floors. Unglazed porcelain tiles are made with clay and feldspar that often is mixed with mineral oxide pigments to produce beautiful, muted colors.

• *Glazed* floor tile has a ceramic coating bonded to a clay body during a kiln firing. The glazing permits the tile to be virtually any color or texture imaginable and presents enormous design possibilities. Because the manufacturing process is usually simple, glazed tiles are relatively inexpensive. Most glazed flooring tiles are impervious to water, stains, and abrasions and are easy to maintain.

Stone

Stone typically is available as cut tiles in standard square dimensions—8×8, 12×12, and 16×16 are popular sizes. The tiles are made by slicing rocks or boulders into thin sheets. The surfaces are left naturally rough, called cleft or split face; honed to a dull finish with a uniform thickness; or polished to glasslike smoothness. Polished stones are more prone to scratches that eventually dull the surface, requiring periodic repolishing to maintain their glossy appearance.

Unlike ceramic tile, which is manufactured to meet certain tolerances and strengths, stone contains soft spots, cracks, and other imperfections that usually are considered to be part of the charm and character of this type of material. Some types of stone, such as granite, are extremely hard, durable, and stain-resistant. Others, such as limestone, are much softer. Softer stones are prone to scratches and must be sealed to protect against stains. Agglomerated stone tiles are made from chips and dust left from

◄ *Coral- and peach-tone Mexican pavers provide visual continuity—and create an especially beautiful floor—that ties this renovated kitchen to the spacious, semicircular add-on breakfast sunroom.*

cutting and processing various natural stone products. The waste material is bonded with a resin to make individual tiles that are then honed or polished.

When selecting stone, confer with a knowledgeable supplier about the various types of stone, the individual characteristics of each type, and the maintenance requirements.

Brick

Brick is another material traditionally associated with sunrooms. It is tough, durable, and a good transition material between outdoors and interior rooms. It is especially appropriate for sunrooms on grade, where it can be used for interior floors as well as surrounding exterior patio surfaces. Install brick over raised wood subfloors, concrete slabs, or directly on grade over a carefully prepared bed of compacted sand.

Brick is available in hundreds of colors and textures. It is rated SW for severe weathering, MW for moderate weathering, and NW for nonweathering, interior-only applications. For floors, specify paver material that has been specially manufactured to withstand the rigors of constant foot traffic. Half bricks—low-profile paver bricks about 1 inch thick—are particularly good for floor installations. They are easier to handle and can generally be installed faster than full-size brick. They reduce the overall weight of the floor, an especially important factor for brick floors installed on raised wood subfloor systems (see Masonry on Wood Subfloors, *opposite*).

Once installed, brick flooring requires periodic maintenance to prevent

◄ *As beautiful as they are practical, terra-cotta quarry tiles provide a durable flooring surface for sunrooms. The rustic appearance and warm, natural earthy colors are especially appealing in this elegant all-glass conservatory. Sealing quarry tiles to prevent staining is recommended.*

staining. Use a good quality brick sealer once each year.

Sheet Vinyl and Vinyl Tile

Vinyl floor coverings are tough, moisture- and stain-resistant, and suitable for sunroom floors. They can be installed on plywood subfloors or directly over a concrete slab that has been properly

MASONRY ON WOOD SUBFLOORS

Brick, stone, and ceramic tiles installed on a raised wood subfloor system need a firm, stable base to handle the considerable weight and prevent flexing of the floor, which could lead to cracked materials or failed grout. This may require strengthening the system by doubling joists, adding support posts and piers, and making sure that the subfloor is not less than 1¼ inches thick by adding a second layer of plywood or a layer of cement backer board. If masonry floors are part of your sunroom plans, make sure a qualified contractor or architect helps you determine the proper load-bearing capacity of your wood subfloor system.

cured and has a completely smooth surface that is free from defects such as cracks and chips. Both sheet vinyl and vinyl tiles are made in a wide variety of colors and patterns to match any decor.

Vinyl flooring is either rotogravure or inlaid. Rotogravure vinyl has a textured surface, and the color and pattern is printed onto the top of the material. The wear layer—the top protective coating—is usually 10–15 millimeters thick. It is less expensive than inlaid vinyl, which features color that extends all the way through the thickness of the vinyl and has a wear layer 25–30 millimeters thick. Inlaid vinyl is more durable than rotogravure.

Sheet vinyl is sold in 6- and 12-foot widths. The wider material means fewer seams are needed for the installation. One drawback of sheet vinyl is that damage is difficult to repair or conceal. It's much easier to replace one or two damaged vinyl tiles. However, tiles have many seams that can trap dirt or allow moisture to get through to the subfloor.

These tiles are not a good choice for high-traffic floors or for floors where spills are likely, such as a greenhouse.

Wood

Wood flooring comes in two basic types. Solid wood flooring is one of the most popular choices for home use and features tongue-and-groove strips or planks of various types of woods, usually oak or maple. More exotic woods such as cherry, ash, or walnut cost about 30 percent more than traditional oak and maple. Solid wood flooring is produced in 2- to 3-inch-wide strips or 4- to 8-inch-wide planks that are either unfinished or prefinished at the factory with coats of tough polyurethane. It must be nailed or screwed to a subfloor—such as plywood. Solid wood flooring is not water-resistant and is not recommended where moisture may be present, such as the floor of a greenhouse.

Engineered wood consists of a top veneer layer of hardwood laminated to two or three layers of softwood, much like plywood. Because of the waterproof resin glue used to bond the layers and the alternating grain direction of each layer, engineered wood is much more stable and moisture-resistant than solid wood flooring. Depending on the type of product, engineered wood is either nailed down or glued directly to the subfloor. Products designed to be glued can be installed on top of a concrete slab. Some wood flooring products are installed as "floating floors." The individual pieces are glued only to each other at the edges, and the flooring is laid over a thin foam mat that absorbs footfalls and prevents the glued joints from cracking. Engineered wood is a good choice for sunrooms because of its resistance to moisture and its ability to remain stable even when temperatures fluctuate.

Plastic Laminate

Plastic laminate flooring was introduced to the U.S. building market in the mid-1990s. It is tough, durable, and resistant to moisture. It has a decorative wear layer that is bonded under pressure to a rigid core of fiberboard or particleboard. A backing material such as kraft paper or foil is added to prevent warping. A coating of aluminum oxide helps laminate flooring resist scratches, dents, stains, fading caused by sunlight, even burns from cigarettes or hot ashes. The top wear layer is created from a photographic image, allowing laminate flooring to closely mimic a variety of woods, stone, or tile. Quality varies, so compare guarantees when shopping. The best-quality floors are warranted against defects, wear, fading, stains, and water damage for 25 years or more. Less-expensive laminate floors have 10-year guarantees.

Plastic laminate flooring installs as a floating floor—individual pieces are edge-glued only to each other and the flooring is laid over a thin foam mat. This type of flooring installs over any firm base and can be installed directly over old flooring materials such as tile, wood, or vinyl.

Concrete

Concrete is an increasingly popular choice for floors that are built directly on grade. There's no need for the additional expense of flooring materials. However, the concrete should be properly prepared to serve as a finished floor. This usually means the top surface is troweled repeatedly while it is still wet to produce a smooth, even finish.

To control cracking, concrete slabs should include seams and control joints. Seams are ½-inch-deep grooves tooled into the surface of the concrete while it is still wet. Seams should be spaced every 3 or 4 feet throughout the slab. Plan carefully to ensure that the seams are integral to the design of the flooring. Control joints prevent cracks caused by the expansion and contraction of the slab due to

MATERIAL	ADVANTAGES	DISADVANTAGES	COSTS
WOOD	Warm, natural appearance. Good for people with allergies.	Moderately expensive. Not good for areas where spills may occur. Needs maintenance.	$5–$10 per sq. ft. Add $2–$3 per sq. ft. for labor.
ENGINEERED WOOD	Has the beauty of wood but is more stable. Resists spills and moisture. Installs over many substrates.	Moderately expensive. Can't be refinished.	$4–$6 per sq. ft. Add $1–$2 per sq. ft. for labor.
LAMINATE	Looks like natural materials. Highly durable and resistant to stains and moisture. Installs over many substrates.	Cannot be refinished. Sometimes sounds hollow underfoot.	$3–$7 per sq. ft. Add $2–$4 per sq. ft. for labor.
VINYL	Durable and moisture-resistant. Easy to clean. Less expensive than most other flooring choices.	Difficult or impossible to repair. Seams may permit moisture to reach subfloor.	$10–$15 per sq. yd. for rotogravure; $25–$35 per sq. yd. for inlaid. Add $2 per sq. yd. for labor.
CERAMIC TILE	Durable and low maintenance. Classic good looks. High moisture resistance.	May be cold to the touch. Unforgiving of dropped objects. Grout lines sometimes hard to clean. Moderately expensive.	The price varies widely, from $1 per sq. ft. to hundreds of dollars for custom types. Add $1–$5 per sq. ft. for labor.
STONE	Unmatched natural elegance. Almost indestructible.	Susceptible to imperfections such as cracks. Must be properly sealed. Expensive.	The price varies widely, from $1 per sq. ft. to hundreds of dollars for rare types. Add $1–$5 per sq. ft. for labor.
CONCRETE	Simple material. Extremely durable and long-lasting. Eliminates need for other finish materials.	Plain, industrial look of ordinary concrete may require additional labor for coloring or painting.	$4–$10 per sq. ft., installed. Coloring or acid etching is additional.
CARPET	Warm, inviting look. Moderately priced. Readily available.	Shows dirt in high-traffic areas. Only certain carpets are resistant to fading from sunlight.	$15–$150 per sq. yd., including installation and pad. Moving furniture is extra.

and worked in with a trowel. Another popular method is to etch the concrete with an acid solution. For this method to work, the concrete must be cured for at least 30 days. The acid is used with pigmented coloring agents that soak into the concrete and produce a mottled, weathered look. Acid etching creates interesting textures and patterns, but the results are difficult to control. To paint concrete, choose long-wearing enamel specifically formulated for concrete floors.

After the surface is smoothed, cured, and prepared, the concrete should be sealed to protect it from spills and stains. Concrete sealer lasts many years between applications.

Carpet

Few floor finishes are as warm and inviting as carpet. It comes in an enormous array of colors, styles, and degrees of quality. New technologies make carpets more stain-resistant, longer-wearing, and easier than ever to clean.

In sunrooms, resistance to fading caused by the sun's ultraviolet light is an important consideration. Carpets made from olefin are the most resistant to fading. Solution-dyed nylon also resists fading, but it is generally available only as a commercial-grade carpet.

Carpet is made from either natural or synthetic fibers. The type of fibers and the construction of the carpet determine its long-term performance.
• *Nylon* is the most popular type of carpet. It is wear-resistant, moderately priced, and available in many colors.
• *Olefin* resists staining, is color-fast, and cleans easily. It has notable resistance to moisture and mildew and is used for indoor and outdoor installations. Berber-type carpets are often made of olefin.
• *Polyester* is noted for its luxurious, soft feel, especially in varieties that feature thick, cut-pile textures. It's easily cleaned and moderately resistant to staining.
• *Acrylic* mimics wool in texture and appearance for a much lower price. It is mildew-resistant and is often used to make bathroom and small throw rugs.
• *Wool* is soft, resilient, and noted for its overall excellent performance. It is often dyed in soft, natural colors that are costly to produce and generally not available on synthetic carpets. Wool typically is more expensive than other carpets.

▲ *Concrete floors are durable and easily maintained. With staining techniques, they can be as beautiful as ceramic tile floors at a fraction of the cost. The staining can produce intricate patterns, such as the mottled earth tones shown here. There are three techniques: Integral colors are raw pigments mixed into the concrete before it is poured; dry-shake hardeners are sprinkled onto the wet surface of newly poured concrete; chemical stains are used on existing slabs. Staining is a difficult process and the results are hard to predict. Hire a professional who has experience staining concrete.*

temperature variations. They go all the way through the concrete and are spaced every 10 or 12 feet. Typically, pressure-treated wood or felt spacers are used to make control joints. The spacer material remains in the slab.

Concrete can be dyed, painted, or acid-etched to produce a variety of interesting patterns and hues. To dye concrete, the coloring agent is added while the concrete is being mixed. This produces permanent, muted colors that extend all the way through the material. Concrete can also be colored after it is poured. Once the concrete is smoothed, a powdered color additive is sprinkled onto the surface

Installing a Prefab Sunroom

A prefabricated sunroom can be constructed in as little as two days, depending on the size and complexity of the unit. Modular parts and framing systems simplify the process; however, the project has many facets: planning an appropriate location for the sunroom, preparing the site, laying out and pouring the foundation, demolishing a portion of an existing exterior wall to provide access, and determining supplemental heating and cooling requirements. Your sunroom dealer should recommend a construction crew that is familiar with the techniques required by your type of unit, as well as a qualified contractor or subcontractors that can handle all other aspects of the job.

> ▼ *This sunroom is set on a low brick curb wall designed to match the existing brick veneer of the house. Creating a sense of architectural harmony is especially important when adding a sunroom to an older or a historic home. (from Four Seasons)*

The type of foundation depends on the style of the sunroom and its position in relationship to your home. Grade-level sunrooms are built on slab or perimeter foundations. Typically, this type of construction includes a short perimeter wall, sometimes known as a knee or dwarf wall, that extends two to three feet above the foundation. The dwarf wall serves to raise the sunroom off the ground,

making the joint between the unit and the foundation less susceptible to infiltration from rain or melting snow. The wall is made of cement block or wood framing and often is veneered with masonry or siding that matches the existing siding of the house. A dwarf wall provides a convenient place to run electrical circuits or baseboard heaters or other types of supplemental heating and cooling devices. Wood platform foundation systems usually are used to bring a sunroom floor up to the level of an existing floor (see Flooring, pages 75–81).

Once the planning is concluded and site preparation and foundation work are completed, an access door or passageway is created between the

This glass room was custom-made to an architect's specifications by a sunroom manufacturer. The slope of the roof echoes that of the main house. The enclosure is snuggled up to an addition that borrows key elements— stucco walls and clay tile roofing. (from Four Seasons)

house and the sunroom. Opening a portion of an exterior wall typically means providing temporary support for rafters or ceiling joists, disconnecting wires and pipes that run through the wall, and cutting through framing members and siding. Demolition work can be noisy, messy, and intrusive on your daily routine. Make sure your contractor is prepared to hang plastic dust curtains to protect your interiors from dirt and grime during the work. Also, make sure the contractor will adequately seal the resulting hole after work is completed so that it is secure and weatherproof. In some situations—especially when there is room to set up ladders and scaffolding, to carry materials, and to move about freely—it is possible to completely install the sunroom shell before opening the wall. This way, the opening is fully protected and secure during the renovation. Some contractors prefer not to proceed this way, however, because the ongoing work is potentially damaging to the sunroom structure.

The complete installation of a moderately sized, prefabricated sunroom costs between $15,000 and $20,000. The smallest versions cost about $8,000.

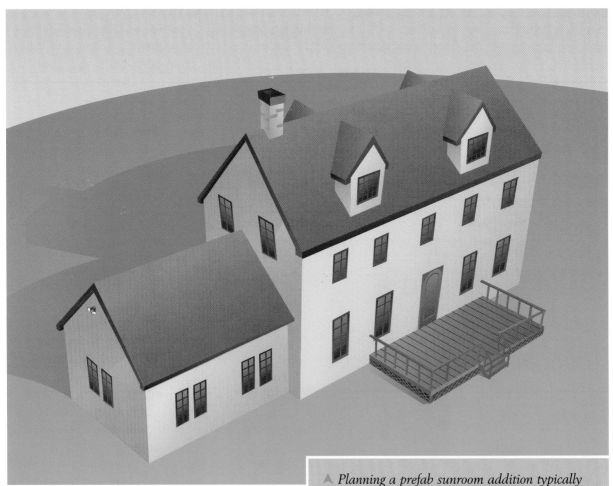

▲ *Planning a prefab sunroom addition typically takes advantage of existing openings to preserve traffic patterns. In this example, the deck will be removed to make way for the sunroom. The doorway will be enlarged during the process.*

▲ After the existing deck is removed, the foundation is laid out. Block doors to prevent accidents.

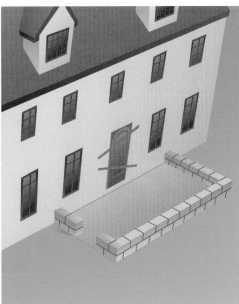

▲ A low perimeter foundation wall is one option for supporting the walls of a prefab sunroom.

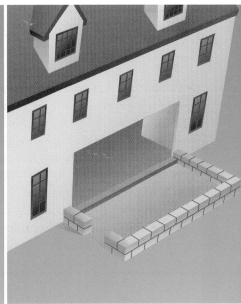

▲ With the foundation set to receive the sunroom, the doorway opening can be enlarged to better incorporate the new living area.

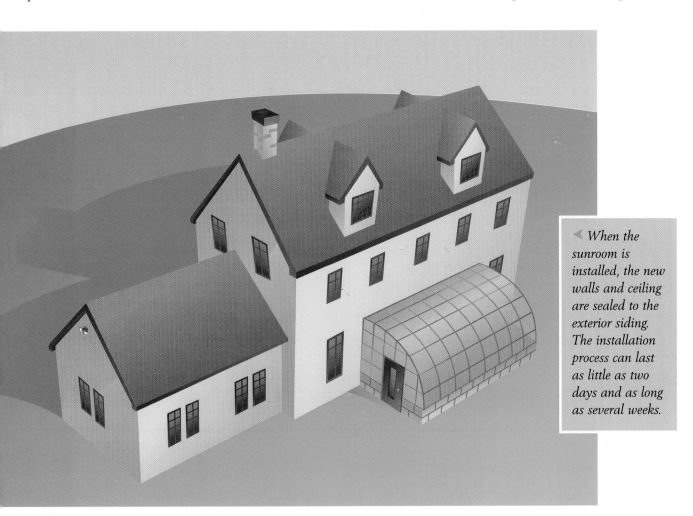

◀ When the sunroom is installed, the new walls and ceiling are sealed to the exterior siding. The installation process can last as little as two days and as long as several weeks.

Planning with a Purpose

Establishing clear goals is the key to a great project.

Make sure your porch or sunroom fulfills your expectations by planning carefully. Thorough planning means setting clear and realistic goals, establishing a budget, being familiar with the construction process, and making informed decisions that keep the project running smoothly.

Planning proceeds in stages. First, define your primary goals. Your definition should include ideas of how you'd like to use the space and how elaborate the finished space will be. The more precise your goals, the more satisfactory the results. For example, increasing your outdoor living space is a good objective, but if you specifically envision summer get-togethers for a group of six to eight people, you can plan a porch big enough for a good-size table and locate it for access to the kitchen or an outdoor cooking area.

Determine the right location for your porch or sunroom by taking into account views, orientation to the sun, and how much privacy you'd like. Be aware of any restrictions imposed by local building departments and codes and how your proposed project will affect existing structures or important landscape features in your yard. Most likely, your project will alter the use of adjacent interior spaces. New doorway locations and altered traffic patterns are a few of the possible considerations. If your new porch or sunroom is part of larger,

◄ *Enclosing an existing deck with a wall composed of windows and French doors brought sunny livability to this California home. An exterior wall between the deck and interior spaces was removed to open up and expand the kitchen. The plan included this small patio area accessible from the new sunroom—creating a natural progression from inside to the outdoor environment.*

> *Before renovating, this architecturally modest colonial-style house displays a typical suburban design. A short breezeway connects the main house and the garage.*

BEFORE

garage

mud rm.

kit.

bkfst.

dining

living

more expansive renovation plans, make sure the new spaces flow easily from one to the other and that all the changes meet your goals for comfort and livability.

As you plan, keep in mind which conveniences would be appropriate. Including several electrical outlets, for example, adds flexibility to the design, making it easy to add or move pole and table lamps, hook up a portable stereo, and plug in a laptop computer. Ceiling fans are a relatively inexpensive way to stir up a breeze to keep the space comfortable. If you like to grow plants in your sunroom, consider plumbing hookups and a floor drain.

Finally, determine what your finished project

will look like. It should be architecturally compatible with the exterior of your home and give the appearance of having been part of the original design—not merely tacked on. Unless you have considerable design experience, consider hiring a professional such as an architect or an experienced member of a design/build team. A professional will help express your ideas on paper and will ensure the project meets local codes, covenants, and setback distances and is structurally sound. A good designer will also harmonize the new spaces with the style of your house and, if necessary, modify your plans to meet the demands of the building site. A qualified architect or designer can actually help

AFTER

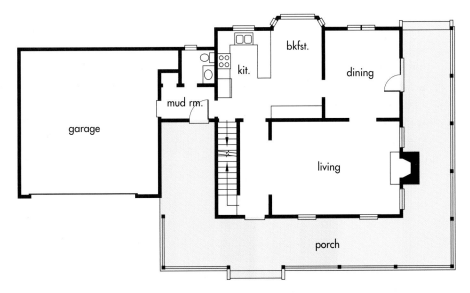

➤ *Building a wraparound porch dramatically alters the exterior appearance, anchoring the house to its site. Besides increasing outdoor living area, two new entrances are added—one to the mudroom and another at the side of the house.*

reduce overall costs by anticipating problems and offering creative solutions before work begins.

Understanding Your Property

Even a small porch must meet all the requirements set by your local planning and zoning commissions. Visit your local planning and zoning offices to pick up a plat—a map that shows your immediate neighborhood, including your property and nearby properties. The plat indicates the size of your lot, its shape, and shows the location of any easements—corridors established on your property that, by law, must be kept free of any structures or impediments. Several types of easements exist.

• Utility easements provide space so that crews can access electrical power lines or other utilities to make repairs. Utility easements typically are situated at the rear of the property and may run the length of the neighborhood. They typically are 5 to 10 feet wide.

• Overland flowage easements include significant depressions or gullies that may collect running water during downpours or when snow melts. These physical characteristics of the land must not be altered or blocked by construction. Flowage easements prohibit structures from being built close to runoff areas where foundations may be undermined or damaged.

89

BEFORE

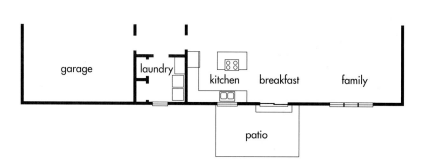

▶ *The rear facade of this two-story house is a blank slate—any well-scaled addition is likely to be an improvement.*

garage   laundry   kitchen   breakfast   family

patio

• Accessibility easements ensure that the property has direct access to a main road or byway. Creating these easements is a common practice when property is split into two parcels, creating a front-facing lot that abuts a road and a rear-facing lot that does not. An accessibility easement guarantees the rear property a corridor—usually wide enough for a driveway—by which a main road is gained.

• Buffer easements are created when a property abuts a public park. The buffer prevents residential construction from intruding on the character of the park.

In addition to easements, most properties are subject to setback requirements—a distance measured from the edges of the property where construction cannot take place. A typical suburban lot may have a front setback of 30–40 feet, side setbacks of 15 feet, and rear setbacks of 10–20 feet. These setbacks include the eaves—a part of the structure that's sometimes overlooked when situating an addition on a piece of property.

When you've finished designing your porch or sunroom addition, the local planning commission requires you to submit a sketch of the site plan for approval. They check the sketch against a plat map to make sure your plans don't intrude on easements or violate setback requirements. Then, the construction plans will be checked by the building department so a building permit can be issued (see The Basics of Building, pages 106–111).

Creating Architectural Harmony

Because porch and sunroom additions alter the exterior appearance of the home, it's important to establish visual harmony between the new structure and the existing. Creating compatibility takes into account many factors, such as the age of the house, the size and shape of the addition, the types of materials used, and the scale and placement of various elements such as windows, posts, and trim. The best designs integrate key landscape features such as driveways, walkways, and plantings.

AFTER

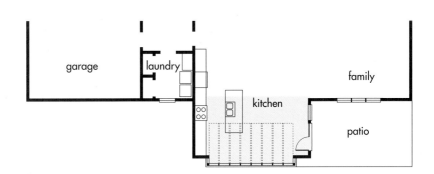

➤ *The small bump-out sunroom is a welcome addition, adding architectural interest and greatly increased living area. In this case, a modest kitchen is expanded into the light-filled chef's dream, complete with skylights and a protected patio.*

Although each house presents unique circumstances, creating harmony follows several basic tenets of good design.

• Don't change styles. A shed-style bump-out sunroom with casement windows would look out of place attached to a colonial-style house with divided-light double-hung windows. Take cues from the existing house. You don't have to reproduce elements precisely, but they should be thoughtfully selected as parts of the entire house. Don't introduce new materials that are radically different from what already exists.

• Pay attention to rooflines. The slope and style of a roof is a major visual element. It should match the existing rooflines. If matching is not practical, then the new roof should be carefully scaled to its addition and maintain harmony with the older roof by using similar materials, fascia treatment, and eaves that echo those appearing on the original house.

• Don't overwhelm the original house. Even if the cost is not a concern and you imagine a grand addition, it should be carefully scaled so that it is in proportion to the main house. Sketching different possibilities on paper allows you to visualize changes and experiment with proportions. Even if you plan to hire a design professional, your sketches are a good way to initiate thoughtful communications about your wishes and needs for the project.

Working with a Design Professional

The job of a professional designer is to create a space that meets your needs. The experience and expertise of professionals allows them to offer fresh ideas, anticipate code restrictions, and deal with unusual problems. If the cost of hiring professionals seems prohibitive, consider that they can help save on overall costs by contributing to the efficiency of the project, organizing and managing work flow, and by helping to avoid expensive mistakes. Many pros are willing to work as consultants for an hourly fee.

When working with professionals, good communication is key to achieving your goals. To help express your ideas, start a clipping folder. Use it to keep articles and photographs from magazines that show ideas and design details that appeal to you. Add product brochures or advertisements that you can share with your designer. Good designers are interested in your lifestyle and should ask questions about how you live, your daily routine, and your project goals.

Three types of design professionals are available for working on porch or sunroom projects. Although they have specialized areas of expertise, most professionals are well versed in all phases of design and can help create a comprehensive plan.

• *Architects* work primarily with structure and reorganization of space. They are familiar with many types of building materials, finishes, and appliances, and have thorough knowledge of structural, electrical, plumbing, heating, ventilation, and air-conditioning systems. Plans that include structural changes to your house and need to be reviewed by your local building and planning commission should bear the stamp of a professional architect or structural engineer. Architects

charge a percentage of the project's total cost, usually 10 to 15 percent. If hired on an hourly basis, they charge $50 to $125 per hour. To find a local architect, look in the Yellow Pages of your phone directory or use the Internet search engine offered by the American Institute of Architects at www.e-architect.com/reference/home.asp.

• *Interior designers* work with colors, wall finishes, fabrics, floor coverings, furnishings, lighting, and accessories to personalize space and create a look that appeals to their clients. Increasingly, interior designers are familiar with building codes and structural requirements and can make recommendations for placement of partition walls, plumbing hookups, electrical outlets, and architectural details such as built-in storage units, moldings, door styles and sizes, and windows. However, project plans might need to be approved by the local building and planning commission, and structural changes must receive the stamp of a structural engineer or registered architect. Extensive remodeling plans may be subject to periodic inspection by the local building inspector. Interior designers certified by the American Society of Interior Designers (ASID) must demonstrate an ongoing

▶ *Gardens are especially important to this green-thumbed homeowner, who purposely planned the entry of his new screen porch to align with a flagstone walkway and an arched arbor passage to the extensive flower beds beyond.*

◀ *Not all additions are welcome. In this example, an above-grade deck is converted to a a plain sunroom (After A). Offsetting the addition (After B) increases architectural interest and preserves the open deck.*

BEFORE

AFTER A

AFTER B

knowledge of materials, building codes, government regulations, safety standards, and the latest products. For more information, visit the ASID website at www.asid.org.

• *Design/build teams* offer complete project management from initial design to completion of construction. Their involvement from the beginning of the project ensures that they are thoroughly familiar with the building methods and techniques specified by the project plan. Design/build teams may not offer the services of a registered architect. Therefore, structural modifications will require the approval of an architect or structural engineer. Design/build teams rarely offer interior design services.

Incorporating Landscaping

Porches and sunrooms are transitional spaces purposely designed to blend with outside environments. Significant landscaping features, such as pathways and patios, should be carefully integrated into the plans for a new space. To plan, sketch your property and the location of your house on graph paper. Note all prominent landscape features. Then establish an outline for your proposed porch or sunroom, taking special care to position doors and stairways. If you have a garden or other type of outdoor space, make sure to establish a sensible, intuitive traffic flow from the new space to the outdoor areas. Computer-based design programs for landscaping are especially useful and feature a variety of ready-made symbols and graphic images of plants and small structures that are easily positioned and edited. Good-quality landscape-design programs are available at computer and electronics stores for $35 to $75.

Certain existing elements, such as large trees and climbing vines, can be integral to your plans. For example, you may decide to position a sunroom so that it will be shaded from western sun by an existing tree. To preserve plantings, instruct your building contractor to use every precaution to protect them. When installing a new foundation and using heavy pieces of equipment, such as a backhoe, a plant's root structure can be irreparably damaged during excavation or when large machines roll over the soil, compacting the earth. Also, trunks may be accidentally bumped, injuring trees.

To protect trees, experts typically recommend building no closer than the tree's drip line—the outer edge of its foliage. Moving a favorite tree out of the way is another option. For $100 to $200, existing trees up to 6 inches in diameter can be transplanted by a tree service equipped with a truck-mounted tree spade. Look in the Yellow Pages of your local telephone directory under "Tree Service" and "Landscape Contractors." For more information specific to your locality and type of tree, contact an agronomist at your state university's agricultural department, or call the horticulturist at your state's Department of Agriculture—if they have the time, they'll provide free advice.

For a fee, you can contract the services of a design professional who specializes in landscaping (see Working with a Design Professional, pages 91–93). A professional will make a map of your property, integrate your proposed project, and produce a plan that is as extensive and complete as you'd like. Landscape architects registered with the American Society of Landscape Architects (ASLA) are usually designers only—the finished plans they furnish must be given to a landscape contractor for installation. Occasionally, a professional landscape architect joins with a landscape contractor to provide full-service planning and installation. An ASLA architect will charge $75 to $125 per hour to inspect and analyze the property and then complete detailed drawings that recommend plantings

and landscape features that connect the new space to the outdoor environment. To create a plan for an average-size suburban house that includes new borders, plantings, a modest patio, and pathways around a new porch or sunroom addition, expect to pay around 15 percent of the cost of the finished landscape project.

Some landscape contractors combine design and installation services, although they may lack the professional certification of the ASLA. Expect to

▼ *When building this lakeside screen porch, views were important. A partial octagon shape takes in the scenery from all angles. Providing electrical outlets and installing a ceiling fan gives this porch basic creature comforts, and leaving the roof rafters exposed preserves the rustic, unpretentious comfort of a cottage in the woods.*

pay $1,000 to $4,000 for a plan and the installation of landscaping features for an average-size suburban house that include new borders, plantings, a modest patio, and pathways around a new porch or sunroom addition.

Adding Electricity

Careful planning of your electrical and lighting requirements guarantees your satisfaction when the project is complete. Having plenty of electrical outlets and adequate lighting provides your new space with the flexibility to meet your needs, no matter how you reconfigure the space or rearrange furnishings.

Adding outlets and fixtures requires calculating your home's existing power requirements to see if you'll need additional circuits to handle the increased load. A licensed electrical contractor will perform these calculations and make sure your project conforms to the specifications set forth by the National Electrical Code (NEC®). According to the Code, there must be one general-purpose circuit, sometimes called a lighting circuit, for every 600 square feet of floor space. Generally, a modest porch addition that includes two or three exterior lighting fixtures, a ceiling fan, and a couple of receptacles can be handled by splicing into an existing circuit. More extensive remodeling probably means adding another general-purpose circuit. Some appliances, such as heaters and air-conditioners, may require their own, separate circuits. If you plan to use your new porch or sunroom as a supplemental kitchen, you will need individual circuits to run small appliances such as cooktops, disposals, and trash compactors. Ceiling

fans are considered as lighting fixtures and do not require a dedicated circuit.

Calculating the electrical requirements of your new project begins at your service panel—where electrical power enters your home and is distributed to individual circuits. Houses built within the last 10 years are likely to have 150- or 200-amp service panels, more than adequate to handle today's power-hungry households. If your house has a 100-amp service panel, however, it may need to be updated.

Splicing into an existing circuit to extend power for a new porch or sunroom means an electrician must locate an existing junction box to add wiring, or else splice in a junction box at some point along the length of existing wiring. Junction boxes often are located in open attic or basement spaces, where they are readily accessible. Occasionally, an electrician must open up walls and ceilings to access wiring and add new junction boxes—work that requires minor demolition. The cost of repairing walls and ceilings must then be added to the cost of the project.

For interior living areas that are used year-round, such as heated sunrooms, most building codes specify that no space along a wall be more than 6 feet from an electrical outlet. Typically, that means each wall includes one or two outlets. If electrical power is furnished by tying into an existing circuit, the NEC advises a total of no more than nine outlets on a 15-amp circuit and no more than 12 outlets on a 20-amp circuit.

There is no minimum number of receptacles for outdoor living areas such as porches. If possible, however, you should include them in your plans—they greatly increase the versatility of your space by allowing you to use lamps, plug in portable stereo equipment or televisions, or work with a portable computer. The easiest way is to locate existing receptacles inside your home, then cut through the exterior siding to install the outdoor receptacles in a back-to-back fashion. The same NEC guidelines outlined above for the total number of outlets per circuit applies. Receptacles for porches should be placed in weatherproof boxes with spring-loaded outlet covers that seal against moisture. Also, most building codes specify that outdoor receptacles be protected by a ground fault circuit interrupter (GFCI). In the event of a short circuit, GFCI-type receptacles detect the deviation in current and instantly shut off power to the receptacle.

As you plan for standard electrical service remember to include plans for telephones and computer modems, cable television hookups, and speaker wires for stereo equipment. These types of wires can be run at the same time as your electrical circuit wires, often using the same access holes in walls and ceilings.

Adding Lights and Fans

Adequate lighting is essential for maximum enjoyment of your space. Most lighting schemes include ambient lighting for general purposes and task lighting for specific needs such as reading or cooking. There also may be accent lighting to illuminate and highlight certain objects such as pieces of art. Have an idea of how you'll use your space so you can install the right lighting.

Enclosed sunrooms have lighting requirements typical to indoor living areas. Provide ambient lighting with recessed ceiling fixtures, track lighting, or wall sconces. Calculate the ambient lighting requirements in lumens—a measure of lighting output. Lumens are listed on the packages that contain light bulbs, but not on the bulbs themselves. A typical 60-watt light bulb produces about 840 lumens. Figure you'll need a minimum of 10 lumens per square foot of living space. For reading and other specific tasks, a floor or table lamp with a 100-watt bulb is ideal. Always refer to the lamp manufacturer's recommendations for the maximum wattage allowed in lighting fixtures. Control lighting with switches placed at entrances and passageways.

Porches represent unique lighting situations. Open porches have few walls to reflect ambient light and are seldom used for tasks requiring specialized lighting. You should have a 60-watt incandescent outdoor lighting fixture on either side of an entry door, located 5 feet, 6 inches above the floor surface. Adding lighting fixtures at 10- to 15-foot intervals along porches provides enough ambient light for safety. If your porch ceiling is enclosed, you can add recessed fixtures. Porch lighting fixtures do not need to be rated for outdoor use if they are

adequately protected by the porch roof—you can even use decorative fixtures, such as chandeliers. Have your outdoor fixtures controlled by switches placed on the wall next to each entry door leading to the porch. For nighttime security, you may want to include lights that are controlled by motion sensors.

Ceiling fans are a popular fixture because they make porch spaces comfortable when the weather is hot and the air is still. Many types of ceiling fans include lights and are controlled either by pull chains or by switches located inside the house. The minimum requirement for headroom beneath a ceiling fan typically is 80 inches.

Setting Budget Priorities

A workable budget usually is a compromise between all the great things you imagine for your finished project and what you're willing to spend to achieve your goals. Your first priority should be to set limits for the total amount of money you'll spend. As a guide, make two lists. One list should include everything you consider essential for your new space. The other list should be the extras—the amenities you'd like to have if there's money left over after you pay for essentials. As you finalize your ideas and move toward construction, request bids from contractors and other professionals you're considering to complete the work. Add a 5 to 10 percent cushion to the total figure to cover probable cost overruns and changes to your plans that may occur after construction has begun. Have a firm idea of what you'd like to spend and convey your goals to the professionals involved in your project. A commitment to your bottom line will help you make the difficult cost-cutting decisions if your project threatens to go over budget.

◀ *This cheery sunroom provides generous amounts of light—both natural and artificial. A partial glass ceiling lets daylight pour inside, while track lights attached to the undersides of the supporting beams are used for both general, ambient lighting and task lighting.*

Furnishing with Style

Today's weather-resistant furnishings and fabrics invite cozy, carefree outdoor living.

Porches and sunrooms are delightful spaces to decorate and furnish. Close to nature and open to plenty of light, these outdoor rooms encourage fresh, inventive, and playful ideas. Hearty, weatherproof surfaces, such as tile floors and walls covered with exterior siding, become a backdrop for upbeat schemes based on comfort and relaxation.

There's no need to compromise your design instincts when it comes to outdoor style—durable, weather-resistant fabrics and furniture are available to match any trend or budget. As with any room, base your design on your intended use of the space. Create groupings for conversation and dining, or establish quiet nooks for solitary reading. Add a hammock or porch swing for simple pleasures. Take care not to clutter traffic patterns. On long, narrow porches, divide the space into several furniture groupings, each united by color and anchored with a handsome rug.

The furnishings should complement the exterior of the house, including the immediate environment. If flower gardens are nearby, you may decide to enhance your surroundings with floral prints and bright splashes of color. Or, place the emphasis on views to the outdoors by keeping furnishings subtle and

◄ An architecturally modest sunroom is transformed into a fresh-air fantasy with gauzy scrim fabric curtains that create a dreamy backdrop and move with the slightest breeze. Light-color linens and a sea-grass rug lend tropical accents that are always in style in outdoor settings. Plenty of potted plants complete the cabanalike tableau.

▲ *Capitalize on the rustic appeal of a porch with exposed rafters and beams by adding vintage furnishings, primitive antiques, and personality-filled accessories. Here, a time-worn pine table and chest mix well with wicker chairs splashed with colorful cushions. A collection of old birdcages emphasizes the open and airy feel of the porch.*

fabrics muted. Roll-up shades, fabric curtains, and blinds made of split bamboo allow you to control sunlight and privacy while adding dashes of personal style. Ornamental trees, climbing vines, and window boxes full of colorful plants or flowers can become integral to the overall design. Remember that windows and doors allow the porch or sunroom to be viewed from adjacent rooms—your new spaces should be a natural extension of your home's interior design.

Outdoor Furniture

True outdoor furniture is manufactured to resist the rigors of radical temperature fluctuations and the onslaught of moisture. These rugged yet beautiful pieces are more popular than ever and are readily available, thanks to an ever-growing interest in outdoor living spaces. They are especially suited for porches, where exposure to the elements is limited but still a real possibility. Styles that range from traditional to contemporary encourage you to express your individuality.

• *Wood* furniture made of teak, redwood, and cypress is weather- and rot-resistant and does not require paints, stains, or other protective coatings. Left to age naturally, these handsome pieces mellow to a silvery gray within a year. They can be left plain or spruced up with mildew-resistant cushions and pillows. Look for brands made from woods harvested in tree farms that are systematically replanted.

Pieces made from average-quality, furniture-grade woods, such as pine, fir, and oak need to be updated yearly with fresh coats of stain, paint, or clear sealer. Oil-based paints are tougher than latex, and gloss finishes last longer than semigloss or flat finishes.

• *Cast-* or *wrought-iron* furniture is heavy and durable but is prone to rust and requires periodic touch-ups and repainting if exposed to the elements. Iron pieces made today are available in many styles, but the material is reminiscent of the graceful, ornate Victorian style of the late 1800s. This type of outdoor furniture is especially appropriate in windy climates, where its considerable weight makes it less prone to being shifted around by gusts.

• *Aluminum* furniture is either wrought or cast in molds. It is rustproof, lightweight, and generally more expensive than iron. Most aluminum furniture comes with tough, baked-on enamel finishes. When shopping, look for thick, heavy-gauge alloys and smooth seams on welded joints. Less expensive versions feature hollow, tubular frames.

• *Plastic* furniture is inexpensive and offered in a limited choice of styles and colors; however, a low-cost set of stacking plastic chairs adds flexibility for entertaining. When buying plastic furniture, look for the best quality—top-grade plastic furniture has a 10-year warranty. Some plastic furniture is made from recycled materials. It is thick, heavy, and looks like wood, but it never needs to be painted.

• *Wicker* furniture has long been synonymous with gracious outdoor style. Elegantly shaped and comfortably familiar, wicker has been popular on porches, sunrooms, and in outdoor living areas for more than a century. Natural wicker is produced in warm browns or is stained with accent colors that are traditionally black or green. Natural wicker may be unfinished or sealed with marine varnish. Painted wicker is usually white. Wicker furniture should not be exposed to the elements. Use it only under a sheltering roof and bring it indoors for storage before cold weather sets in. Take especially good care of antique wicker (see Caring for Wicker, *right*). Weatherproof wicker is made of moisture-proof polyester resins and rustproof aluminum framing. Colors mimic those of natural wicker, but they can be placed outdoors and exposed to the elements without damage. It is slightly more expensive than comparable pieces made of natural wicker.

• *Twig* furniture is usually made from green willow branches that are bent into sweeping curves and decorative curlicues to form the arms, legs, and backs of the pieces. The frames are weather-resistant, but keeping twig furniture under shelter prolongs its life. Exposure to direct sun may cause rapid shrinking of the branches, which tends to loosen fasteners. Twig furniture has a carefree, rustic appeal that works well with cushions and pillows in bold colors and patterns. It often is produced locally—look for good prices on twig furniture at area crafts shops, farmers' markets, and roadside stands.

CARING FOR WICKER

Wicker furniture needs regular maintenance and cleaning, especially because dust and dirt tend to gather in the tiny crevices formed by the fiber cords. Occasionally vacuum wicker pieces thoroughly using a brush attachment. Once a year, clean wicker with a soft bristle brush or a sponge—never a plastic pot scrubber—and an oil soap. Rinse thoroughly and wipe dry with clean, soft towels.

Wicker fibers must be slightly moist to remain pliable. If they dry out, they can become brittle and break. Unpainted, unfinished wicker should be misted occasionally to keep the fibers from drying out. Keep painted wicker in good repair by repainting it every two or three years with a top-quality exterior paint. Remember, however, that painting or varnishing an antique piece of wicker will diminish its value.

Fabrics

Today's weather-resistant materials provide great outdoor style. Some synthetic fabrics faithfully reproduce the look and feel of natural fibers such as canvas and resist mold, mildew, and fading. Use them for cushions, pillows, and curtains to brighten and energize porches and sunrooms. In general, fabrics used outdoors can feature bolder colors and larger patterns than those used indoors.

• *Laminated cotton* is made by coating cotton fabric with acrylic or polyurethane. The result is a tough, flexible outdoor material that resists moisture. However, the natural cotton fibers are still prone to fading and mildew spotting, and their use should be limited to sheltered areas. You can waterproof your own fabrics with iron-on vinyl available at fabric stores.

• *Solution-dyed acrylics* dry quickly, resist mildew and fading, and are easily sewn into soft furnishings, pillows, and curtains.

• *Woven polyester* is coated with vinyl to produce an especially strong, durable fabric ideal for umbrellas, hammocks, and seat cushions.

• *Hearty natural fabrics* such as canvas, duck, and twill are strong but only mildly resistant to fading. They can be used for cushions, curtains, shades, and slipcovers, but they are prone to mildew—make sure they can be easily removed for cleaning.

Shades, Blinds, and Curtains

Window treatments give porches and sunrooms a touch of elegance and romance. They soften large amounts of hard glass surfaces, provide privacy, and help to control excessive light and glare. Any traditional window treatment will work in a sunroom, but hot, bright sun can quickly pale the colors in fabrics that are not especially made to resist fading. On porches, billowing fabric curtains add swaths of color and a refined—yet fun—sense of style to living areas that are completely open to the outdoors. Sheer cotton panels add a dreamy background.

HANGING A PORCH SWING

Porch swings provide cherished images of relaxed, easygoing summer days. Some folks wouldn't think of having a porch without one. To install a porch swing, you need access to a roof rafter. Unless you have thick beams supporting your roof, you probably need to strengthen the rafter by "sistering" it—adding a companion rafter alongside and bolting the two together. The sister rafter must sit on the same support points as the original rafter. To hang the swing, drill through both rafters and install eye bolts parallel to the floor. Adjust the seat height with the chains provided with the swing. Don't use eye screws installed vertically—directly up from underneath. Even if it feels solid, in the long run that type of a connection is not secure enough to be safe.

When positioning the swing, make sure it has enough clearance front and back to move freely. Keep the front of the swing clear of tables and accessories. Instead, place serving tables to the side to hold books or refreshing glasses of lemonade.

▶ *Views from this screen porch are framed by a colorful valance made from green-and-white stripe cotton fabric edged with blue ribbon and cut into long Gothic points. The fabric is treated to resist moisture. Pine furniture and a big twig settee provide character. To add vibrant color, the concrete floor is painted to resemble a kilim rug.*

Cotton sheets make simple, low-cost curtains. They come in a variety of colors and prints, but since sheets aren't designed for direct exposure to sunlight, don't expect colors to last very long. Shower curtains also work well—they are durable, moisture-resistant, and have many colors and textures. Split bamboo and matchstick blinds are popular choices—the natural wood tones blend readily with a variety of design schemes. Used on a porch, blinds made of wood should be coated with a clear, penetrating wood sealer prior to installation to prevent staining and mildew.

Rugs

Rugs provide splashes of color and soften the look and feel of hard surface floorings such as ceramic tile or concrete. Although you can use any type of rug in a porch or sunroom, remember that these environments are prone to dirt and grime tracked in from the outdoors. Choose moderately priced hurries, kilims, or woven rag rugs that are colorful, durable, and easy to clean. Rugs of sisal or hemp are naturally resistant to moisture and have a casual appearance that blends well with most porch or sunroom groupings. Acrylic rugs are easy to care for and resist fading. For high-traffic areas, select a piece of indoor/outdoor carpeting and have all the edges bound.

▼ *With touches of classic lakeside vernacular, this rustic porch features posts made from unpeeled birch logs. To comply with building codes, structural lumber is in place just behind the logs. Striped camp-style awnings, wool throws with traditional American Indian designs, and stick furniture are right at home in this woodsy setting.*

The Basics of Building

Understanding construction keeps your project efficient.

Knowing the techniques and procedures required for construction allows you to establish effective communications with your architect, general contractor, and other professionals. Good communication helps to keep the job on time and on budget. If you do the work yourself, learning about the building process familiarizes you with materials and the sequence of events so you can make informed decisions.

Finding and hiring the right contractor for the job is also a process.

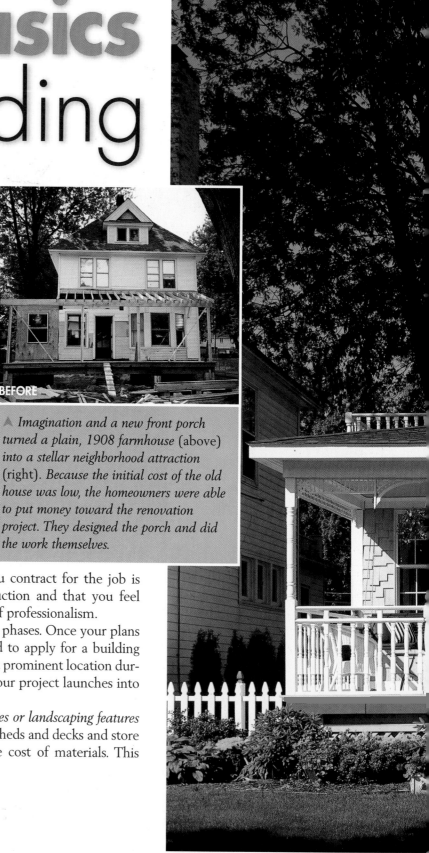

BEFORE

▲ *Imagination and a new front porch turned a plain, 1908 farmhouse* (above) *into a stellar neighborhood attraction* (right). *Because the initial cost of the old house was low, the homeowners were able to put money toward the renovation project. They designed the porch and did the work themselves.*

Take the time to make sure the team you contract for the job is familiar with porch and sunroom construction and that you feel comfortable with their abilities and level of professionalism.

A porch or sunroom project has several phases. Once your plans are approved, you or your contractor need to apply for a building permit. The permit should be displayed in a prominent location during construction. With a permit secured, your project launches into several phases of construction including:

• *Preparing the site by removing old structures or landscaping features that may be in the way.* Dismantle existing sheds and decks and store the lumber for future use—saving on the cost of materials. This

BEFORE

phase should be considered carefully—know exactly which plantings are expendable and which you'd like to move to a safe location. If trees are nearby, instruct your contractor to make every effort to preserve them during construction.

• *Excavating the site and installing a foundation.* Most building codes require any new structure attached to a house to be supported by a foundation that extends below the frost line. In most areas of the country, this means the foundation footing must be 36 to 48 inches below grade. Before digging a trench for the foundation, you or your contractor must contact all local utility companies to determine the location of any underground gas, water, sewer, electrical power, cable television, and telephone lines. If any of these services are in the path of the excavation, they must be shut off and rerouted. Coordinate this phase carefully so you'll know exactly when the services are to be shut off and how long the disruption will last. Once the foundation is installed, expect a pause in construction of one to three days while the concrete cures.

• *Framing the flooring system, stairs, railings, walls, and the roof.* This part of the construction should be straightforward and proceed without interruption.

• *Creating any new entrances or passageways by removing or opening up existing walls.* This kind of demolition work is the messiest and most disruptive of normal household activities. Depending on the scope of your project, you may have a ragged opening in your house walls for days or even weeks. Make sure to discuss with your contractor before work begins exactly how they plan to open up the house and what precautions they will take to prevent dirt and dust from entering living areas. Typically, contractors hang clear plastic dust curtains around the immediate construction area. However, it's not a foolproof guarantee against dust. Protect valuable or hard-to-clean furnishings by draping them with sheets. If the crew needs access to a bathroom, cover flooring with plastic floor protectors made specifically for construction sites. Your

◄ *To design a porch for this older house* (left), *the owners snapped pictures of neighborhood houses with porches they liked. Using a computer, they superimposed their favorites on a photo of their existing house until they had a winner.*

109

contractor should have plans for securing any openings each evening after the day's work is complete. Usually, sheets of plywood are temporarily nailed in place to keep out weather and to block entry.

• *Installing electrical wiring, plumbing, insulation, lighting fixtures, and heating and cooling systems.* This work is done after the structure is framed and before it is enclosed with wall finish materials. Walls are left open until an official building inspector has toured the site and declared the work to be sound, safe, and in accordance with all local building codes.

• *Installing appliances, fixtures, and adding finish materials and trim to walls and ceilings.* Depending on the complexity of design, installing trims and decorative details typically is slow-paced, deliberate work. At this stage, your desire to see construction completed may make the process seem agonizingly slow. Ask your contractor for a firm estimate of when the work is to be completed.

• *Installing new landscaping features.* Much of this work can be initiated and completed while construction work is progressing. However, it is vital that your building contractor and landscape contractor coordinate their efforts so they won't get in each other's way.

Hiring a Contractor

Unless you are an accomplished do-it-yourselfer with plenty of time to devote to a project, hire a professional building contractor. Selecting a contractor is one of the most important aspects of getting your project done to your satisfaction. Take the time necessary to choose a contractor who has a good reputation and with whom you feel comfortable.

A licensed contractor is someone who has completed state requirements to perform various types of work. General contractors usually have a broad knowledge of all aspects of construction and are hired to organize and complete a job according to an agreed-upon schedule. Specific types of contractors are also called subcontractors. Electrical contractors, for example, have passed state certification programs that permit them to perform work relating to electrical hookups. It is the responsibility of your general contractor to hire all subcontractors necessary for the completion of your project. A good general contractor has established relationships with many reliable subcontractors and can be counted on to furnish top-quality work that is completed in a timely fashion.

To find a qualified general contractor:

• Ask friends, neighbors, colleagues, or professional acquaintances for names of reliable contractors. Be sure you get several recommendations.

• Meet with prospective contractors to discuss your project. Ask about their experience remodeling porches and sunrooms and what problems they encountered. Don't hesitate to ask for a ballpark figure for your project. A ballpark figure isn't a precise bid and should not be regarded as an agreement of any kind, but discussing money at an early stage may give you an idea of how knowledgeable a contractor is and how comfortable he or she is discussing costs.

Ask how long they have been in business and if they carry insurance. Without insurance, you are liable for accidents that occur on your property. Contractors should have a certificate of insurance to cover damage, liability, and workers' compensation. It is an acceptable part of the process to request that you see the certificate before proceeding.

• Obtain references from contractors and take the time to inspect their work. Reliable contractors should provide this information readily and will be proud to have their work on display. Check with your local Better Business Bureau to see if any complaints have been filed about your candidates.

• Narrow your choices—select three to five contractors—and ask for final bids. Make sure all contractors have similar deadlines for submitting bids—about three weeks should be sufficient. Eliminate from contention any contractor who posts a late bid without a reasonable excuse for doing so; having too much work is not a valid excuse.

• Review each bid carefully to see how thoroughly the bids have been researched. A bid should include itemized lists of materials, itemized figures for installation work, a timeline with stages of completion clearly defined, and an amount specified for the contractor's fee—usually 10 to 15 percent of the total costs. The best contractors offer a penalty for work that is not completed in a reasonable amount of time. There should also be an agreed-upon rate for change orders. Change orders occur when the homeowner decides to make alterations to the plan or to the type of materials specified. Although most contractors will work with clients to make minor changes, some alterations cause work delays that disrupt shipping arrangements or cause contractors to alter schedules with other jobs. The best way to avoid changes is to plan thoroughly, well in advance.

• When it comes to a final selection, take all factors into account, including price. Be skeptical of any bid that seems significantly lower than others—the lowest bidder is not always the one who will give the most satisfying results.

• Once you find your contractor, you should make an effort to keep lines of communication open. Schedule regular meetings to discuss progress and keep informed of interim deadlines. Tell your contractor that you don't expect to make your final payment until the job has passed all required building inspections, you have seen written proof that all subcontractors and suppliers have been paid, and you and your contractor have walked through the project and agreed that the job is complete.

Getting Bids

Getting bids is not just the job of your contractor—you have responsibilities, too. Your duty is to furnish detailed blueprint drawings and a materials list. Blueprints are produced by a registered architect, but a qualified designer or even the homeowner can create usable plans. Blueprints from a registered architect can be given directly to a contractor for bids, but plans produced by a designer or the homeowner must first be reviewed, approved, and stamped by a registered structural engineer.

The materials list should be as complete and comprehensive as possible. It should specify the quantity and brand names of materials needed and the brand names and model numbers of fixtures and appliances that are to be installed. If specific companies are not identified, the contractor will furnish brands of his or her preference.

Many homeowners enjoy being involved in the selection process and like to shop for certain items themselves. Be sure your contractor understands your intentions and the materials list indicates any purchases you intend to make. Both you and your contractor must agree about any possible limitations due to size, weight, and other relevant factors.

When bids start to arrive, study them to see how each was prepared and the level of detail each contractor provides. A meticulously prepared bid usually indicates that the contractor has given careful consideration to your project and is prepared for potential problems. If all the bids vary widely, review each bid with the contractor who prepared it to discover why. It may be that certain items or tasks have been omitted. Make sure all the prospective contractors are working with identical information about your plans.

Making a Contract

Once you have made your selection, you should sign a written contract with your contractor. Many contractors have prepared forms. If you are unsure about the specific points of a contract, you should consult with a lawyer before proceeding.

Contracts are not all alike; however, a good contract should cover these points:
• A precise description of all work to be completed by the contractor and subcontractors and a description of all materials to be installed.
• The total cost of the job including all materials, labor, and fees.
• A schedule of payments that you will make to the contractor. Be wary of contracts asking for large up-front payments—some states even limit the amount of up-front payments made to contractors before work begins.
• A work schedule with calendar dates specified for the completion of each stage of the project. The schedule should include an allowance for delays due to delivery problems, weather-related interruptions, and back orders of scarce products.
• A "right of recision" that allows homeowners to back out of the contract within 72 hours of signing.
• A certificate of insurance that guarantees the contractor has the appropriate insurance.
• A warranty that guarantees that the labor and materials are free from defects for a certain period of time, usually one year.
• An arbitration clause that specifies the method that you will use to settle any disputes.
• A description of change-order procedures stating what will happen if you decide to alter the plans or specifications after the contract has been signed. The description should include a fee structure for change requests.
• A release of liens to assure the homeowners won't incur liens or charges against the property as a result of legal actions filed against the contractor or any of the subcontractors hired.

Index

Numbers in **BOLD** indicate pages with photographs.